WORSHIP IN E

Worship in Every Event

Worship Resources for Every Day

Tony Jasper
and
Pauline Webb

OXFORD UNIVERSITY PRESS

1998

Oxford University Press, Great Clarendon Street, Oxford OX2 6DP

Oxford New York

Athens Auckland Bangkok Bogota Bombay Buenos Aires
Calcutta Cape Town Dar es Salaam Delhi Florence Hong Kong Istanbul
Karachi Kuala Lumpur Madras Madrid Melbourne Mexico City
Nairobi Paris Singapore Taipei Tokyo Toronto Warsaw

and associated companies in
Berlin Ibadan

Oxford is a trade mark of Oxford University Press

British Library Cataloguing in Publication Data

Data available

ISBN 0–19–145695–0

1 3 5 7 9 10 8 6 4 2

Typeset in Times New Roman by The Spartan Press Ltd, Lymington, Hants
Printed in Great Britain on acid-free paper by
Bookcraft Ltd., Midsomer Norton

Contents

Introduction

This is a book of worship for every day. It is said of George MacLeod, founder of the Iona Community, that he always went to his prayers with a Bible in one hand and a newspaper in the other. Both will be essential resources for those who use this book. It is designed for people who lead short acts of worship at the beginning of gatherings held in the midst of the workaday world such as a regular weekday activity or school assembly, church meeting or works fellowship, training class or house group. Its themes are based on the kinds of news items that dominate our headlines from time to time. The acts of worship that follow reflect on those current events in the light of the Bible and echo their significance in the choice of hymns and in the focus of the prayers and intercessions. The actual headlines used by way of introduction to the service will vary according to what is topical at the time, but a list of possible themes will be found in the contents page, and can be selected to match the events that are of current concern.

The format of the services is based on the 'Act of Worship' broadcast every Friday on BBC Radio 4 from a studio in Manchester, now immediately preceding the 10 a.m. news bulletin. Often there is an item in the day's news which will have been present in people's minds as they have listened to the daily religious service. As far as possible, the presenter in the studio chooses music, readings, and prayers that are most relevant to those concerns. There are constraints of time, in that no service can last longer than fifteen minutes. Within that period it is customary to include a couple of hymns or modern songs, a psalm or anthem, a Bible passage with brief comment, and a period of intercession. Even though the service is on radio, it is felt important that those listening should be encouraged as far as possible to participate in the worship by the use of responsive prayers, antiphonal psalms, and familiar hymns. The same aim has guided the compilers in preparing the services in this volume, for worship is meant to be 'liturgy', literally 'the work of the people'.

For reasons of immediacy and brevity, the services in this book are simple in form, not requiring a great deal of preparation beforehand. But they may on occasions be used as part of a longer service of worship in which there could be fuller participation by the congregation. Worship should never be a passive experience. Movement and music, dance and drama, picture and symbol can all be used to enhance an act of worship, and we invite readers to use their imagination in presenting the themes we suggest in as stimulating a way as possible.

The Aim of Worship

'To worship', wrote William Temple, 'is to quicken the conscience by the holiness of God, to feed the mind with the truth of God, to purge the imagination by the beauty of God, to open the heart to the love of God, to devote the will to the purpose of God.' When we worship, we 'give worth' to God. So we give worth too to all that God has created and to the events through which God speaks to us. We begin to see the world, not as a godforsaken chaos, but as the arena of God's loving activity in which we have our part to play.

Each act of worship begins, therefore, with an act of praise to God. Even when we are surrounded by the direst events which leave us reeling in despair, with many unanswered questions on our lips, and many unspoken doubts in our hearts, we affirm the power of God, and by that affirmation we ourselves are strengthened. The story is told of a group of Jewish prisoners who, whilst suffering in the concentration camps, put God on trial. The accusation was that God had either deserted them or did not exist at all. When the eventual verdict went against God, the rabbi concluded the debate by suggesting that now the matter was settled, the company should turn to their prayers! Those who had most vigorously protested against God's absence now equally reverently joined in the traditional psalms that worshipped God's presence, as though they could behold the beauty of the Lord even in the midst of their prison.

Beholding that beauty does not, however, blind our eyes to the prevailing ugliness. Like Isaiah, who saw the glory of the Lord uplifted in the temple, such a vision can make us even more vividly aware of our own uncleanness and that we 'live among a people of unclean lips'. So we turn from praise to penitence, on our own behalf and on that of the society in which we live. Then, with the cleansing that comes from forgiveness, we are sent back into our world to be the channels of God's grace and the agents of God's kingdom. Thus, worship becomes not a mere ritual of recognition, but also a means of response to God's worth in our world.

The Bible in Worship

The Bible is itself both a worshipful and an eventful book, in the fullest sense of that word. It is a record of what God was saying to the people through the events of their times. 'The word of God *happened* to us', said the prophets, using the Hebrew word 'dabar' (God spoke), but referring to an event rather than merely to a spoken word. 'What we have heard and seen, we declare to you,' proclaimed the evangelists. For them the Word of God had become flesh and dwelt among them, and was incarnate in all the events they experienced in their encounter with Christ. So the Bible is, as P. T. Forsyth has expressed it, 'history preaching'. It is not surprising that its message often has a startling relevance to the history of our own times, where we still see God's love made real through the lives of men and women who serve the society in which they live.

To point up that relevance as clearly as possible, we have chosen to use in this book one of the latest of the modern translations of the Bible, the *New Revised Standard Version* Anglicized Edition, first published by the Oxford University Press in 1995. It has the advantage of including the results of modern biblical scholarship, but at the same time retaining more often than some earlier modern translations, phrases that have a familiar ring about them. For example, unlike some other versions, this one has made no attempt to update the famous, and transparently relevant passage that is inscribed on the wall outside the United Nations Headquarters, prophesying the day when 'They shall beat their swords into ploughshares and their spears into pruning hooks'. Another virtue of this translation is that it has recognized the need to make the language as inclusive as possible: St Paul addresses both *brothers and sisters*, and Jesus calls *any* (not just 'any *man*') who want to be his followers to take up their cross daily and follow him (which is, incidentally, a better translation of the Greek).

It is important that anyone reading the Bible passages aloud to others should take some time in preparing how best they can be read. Some time ago, on Radio 4, readings from the whole Bible were given by professional actors over a cycle of two years. They all took considerable pains to ensure that they understood the proper interpretation of passages before they read them. They knew well how much phrasing, emphasis, and timing can affect the understanding of what is heard. Recordings of those readings are available and are well worth studying by those who have the responsibility of reading the Bible aloud. There is also a dramatized version of the Bible which can be used at times to emphasize more effectively passages of dialogue or dramatic import. In the services in this book, we have recommended that the psalms usually be read antiphonally, as this echoes the original Hebrew poetic form of repetition. This could be done effectively by just two voices, where the group as a whole do not have copies of the text.

Although generally the passages that have been chosen here are relevant to the topical theme of a particular service, in some cases that relevance will need to be pointed up by some introductory comment placing the reading in its own context but referring it also to current events. It is recommended that the comments be kept as short as possible. It is important to let the Bible speak for itself and to give people time, following the reading, to meditate for themselves on its message for today.

Music in Worship

From the earliest records of Christian worship in the New Testament, it is clear that 'hymns and psalms and spiritual songs' were regarded as an essential way of expressing fellowship, of recalling the great events of the past, and of encouraging believers along the way of discipleship. In almost every religious revival since, music has played a major role in celebrating and teaching the faith. In our own time, the outburst of religious music has resulted in a flood of hymn-books and song-sheets pouring into churches, so that leaders of worship can be almost overwhelmed by the abundance of choice. In this book we have chosen all the hymns from the book *BBC Songs of Praise*, published by Oxford University Press and the BBC and based on the television programme of that title. It contains many old favourites as well as modern hymns reflecting contemporary concerns.

One fascinating feature of modern worship is that there has been a universal revival of the ancient custom of singing acclamations such as Hallelujah, and responses such as Kyrie Eleison (Lord, have mercy). Through the influence of the ecumenical movement, where ancient churches of the Eastern tradition meet with the younger churches of the West and the South, Christians have been learning chants from the distant past and lyrics from all parts of the world. Encouraged particularly by the tradition of worship in the ecumenical community at Taizé in France, many haunting melodies set to simple phrases of prayer have now become familiar all over the world. At international ecumenical gatherings of recent years, African, Asian, and Latin American musicians have also enlivened the worship by teaching songs from their own traditions. The words and music for these overseas lyrics and chants can be found in *Worshipping Ecumenically*, published by the World Council of Churches, and the page reference is given on each occasion. One great advantage of such acclamations and lyrics is that people learn them easily without the need for hymn-books. So the singing becomes a link both with the saints of the past, and with the world church of today.

Prayer in Worship

When the disciples asked Jesus to teach them to pray, the model he gave them was a corporate prayer, which begins and ends in the worship of God and includes both personal petition and intercession for others. It is a prayer for the kingdom of God, particularly for evidence of that kingdom here on earth. It is an affirmation that whatever might be happening in the current events of our world, the kingdom and the power and the glory ultimately all belong to God.

The prayers we have prepared for this book are similarly prayers for the kingdom. In one sense they could be called political prayers, as they are based on the belief that prayer is a means of releasing power into the world, and of bringing earthly powers under the scrutiny of God's will. Most of them are prayers that have arisen out of particular situations and in response to immediate needs. But we have tried to bear in mind the fact that prayer is not asking God for what we want, but rather seeking to know what God wants, and then offering our response to what God's will requires of us.

Most of the prayers in this book have been written by the compilers themselves to relate to the particular themes. But we would commend the use of the many excellent books of prayer now available to supplement what we have offered here. Prayers, like letters, can take many different forms. Some letters are simply a means of keeping a relationship strong and close; many of the traditional collects are like that kind of regular communication between the soul and God, and form a fitting opening to an act of worship. Some letters are an attempt to express a love that is difficult to put into words; prayers of adoration, like such letters, turn often to the words of poets and mystics to express the soul's deepest longing. Some letters are a means of sharing a concern for others whose needs have been brought to our notice; in intercession particularly we place before God the needs of those we love and the needs of our world. Beware of turning the time of intercession into a mini-news bulletin. A leader in prayer was once heard to say, 'O God, as you will have read in *The Times* this morning . . . '! We do not need to tell God what is happening, but to ask God's guidance and help for all who are involved.

'We've been prayed for, you know,' replied Archbishop Desmond Tutu when he was asked in a newspaper interview how he accounted for the unexpectedly peaceful transition to democracy in South Africa. To the somewhat bemused reporter, he went on to explain, 'This is a miracle. It is not of our doing. We've been on the intercession list of the world for a heck of a time. Yeah man, it works. It really works!' (*Independent*, 3 October 1994). But, as he readily admitted, many other places have been on the intercession lists of the churches for so long that there are times when the repetition of their names becomes almost like a meaningless litany, with apparently no miraculous result. If the litany becomes meaningless, then the prayer inevitably seems ineffective.

So prayers of intercession need to be supported by the supply of information to those who are being asked to pray, and by continued concern and active commitment to the cause being brought before God. The effectiveness of the prayers for South Africa must have owed much to the vigour of the international Anti-Apartheid Movement, the campaigning of many activists in the churches across the world, and the commitment of thousands of men and women of courage within South Africa itself. So, to supplement the intercessions suggested in this book, we append a list of organizations that can help to provide information and mobilize support for the various issues that become our current themes.

Prayer is a means of bringing others into the presence of God. When people ask for our prayers they are asking for more than kind thoughts or helpful advice; they are seeking a spiritual energy, a sense that they are not alone, that they are upheld by arms of love. Prayer can be that kind of telepathy, sending out waves of compassion which can be tuned into by the spiritually sensitive, just as the radio waves going through the ether can be transmitted to those with the equipment to receive them. There are moving testimonies to the way in which prayer can thus reach into places no other power can reach, making real the presence of God to those otherwise cut off from all communication with the outside world.

The Russian poet, Irina Ratushinskaya, gave evidence of that when she was finally released from a seven-year prison sentence in the Soviet Union. In the strict regime labour camp where she had spent four years, she had been severely treated, chiefly as punishment for her defence of other women prisoners and for her own commitment to the Christian faith. Cut off from her family, she was told by the guards that she was completely forgotten by those outside, though in fact vigils were being kept on her behalf in churches all over the world. Then one day, when she was feeling particularly abandoned in her cold and filthy cell, she suddenly regained her courage. In a radio interview, she described the experience thus: 'In the first part of November I was in the cell on hunger strike, and on the eighth or ninth day—I cannot remember which it was—I felt a strange heat and I understood that there was help for me from all the love of different people from different countries who prayed for me, and thanks to these people I was still alive.' Soon after that she was unexpectedly released. It is because we believe in the power of that kind of concentrated prayer that we hope that the services in this book will be for many but the prelude to vigils of similar concern.

The People at Worship

In preparing this book, we have had in mind several different groups who might make use of it. Some of the services are based on scripts that were used on Radio 4 at times of various emergencies and significant current events. The very nature of radio means that it is difficult to define which people are sharing in the service; but we know that many listen alone in their own homes, or in small groups in hospital or residential homes, whilst others are casual eavesdroppers driving along in their cars or overhearing the radio in their workplaces. There is a well-known anecdote describing how, in the early days of radio, a bishop responded negatively to the thought of broadcasting prayers. 'People might even be listening in saloon bars with their hats on,' he objected. It is hoped that anyone who does eavesdrop on a service of this kind, perhaps as it forms a part of a meeting they are attending which is not primarily devotional, will find it relevant and helpful. Other services in this book have been used in informal weeknight gatherings of young people and reflect the particular concerns that affect their lives. In the appendix we have listed many of the organizations which are particularly able to help young people in need of advice and support.

When we allow the events that so suddenly and tragically engulf our world to set the agenda of our prayers, we shall find that there are occasions when we are so overwhelmed that we cannot find words to express what we want to say. At times like that, we can turn to the reassurance given us in the Letter to the Romans: 'Likewise the Spirit helps us in our weakness; for we do not know how to pray as we ought, but that very Spirit intercedes with sighs too deep for words. And God, who searches the heart, knows what is the mind of the Spirit, because the Spirit intercedes for the saints according to the will of God.' May that Spirit pervade every act of worship, in every event.

January 1998   PAULINE WEBB
                                                       TONY JASPER

ABBREVIATIONS

The following abbreviations have been used for reference throughout the book:

BCP	*Book of Common Prayer*
NEM	*New Every Morning* (BBC)
OBP	*The Oxford Book of Prayer*, ed. George Appleton, (OUP, 1985)
WCC	World Council of Churches
WE	*Worshipping Ecumenically*, ed. Per Harling (WCC, 1995)

All hymn numbers refer to the *BBC Songs of Praise* hymnbook
All chant numbers refer to *Worshipping Ecumenically*

Aids

Today many people are wearing red ribbons. They signify sympathy and support for people who suffer as a result of Aids. The very name of the disease still strikes terror in some hearts. So many myths and unfounded fears have grown up around it. But much more is known now about how it is caused and how it can be prevented, and with continuing research we dare to hope that one day we may know how it can be cured. Meanwhile there are a growing number of organizations who care for its victims and for their families and friends. Each year in Southwark Cathedral a special service is held to mark World Aids Day. In this act of worship we shall use some of the prayers and readings from such a service, prepared by people who themselves suffer from Aids, and by those who befriend them. First, a hymn that expresses the companionship and compassion which those who suffer from Aids so dearly need.

HYMN 374

We cannot measure how you heal

PRAYER

Lord, as we worship today, give us a vision.
Move us by your Spirit.
Bring good news to us all;
Freedom to broken people;
And heaven, here on earth.
Give us a vision that will carry us through
our disappointments and our failures,
our anxious and unhappy times,
and the monotony of boring routines.
**Give us a vision that will lift our lives
and lead us into new ways of service.**

Help us to dare to dream of love
in a world that speaks of hate.
**Help us to dare to dream of hope
in a world that speaks of despair.**

Help us to dare to dream of peace
in a world that speaks of war.
Help our worship today, Lord
Give us vision inspired by your Spirit.

READINGS

Joel 2.28

I will pour out my Spirit upon all flesh; your sons and your
daughters shall prophesy, your old men shall dream dreams, and
your young men shall see visions.

A candle is lit

Response: **Kindle a flame to lighten the dark**
and take all fear away.

Romans 8.18–21

I consider that the sufferings of this present time are not worth
comparing with the glory about to be revealed to us. For the
creation waits with eager longing for the revealing of the children
of God; for the creation was subjected to futility, not of its own but
by the will of the one who subjected it, in hope that the creation
itself will be set free from its bondage to decay and will obtain the
freedom of the glory of the children of God.

A second candle is lit

Response: **Kindle a flame to lighten the dark**
and take all fear away.

INTERCESSIONS

O God, turn your Spirit loose now and us with it, that we may
go to where the edge is, and stand together there with folk with
Aids, and those affected by it; to face with you the shape of our
mortality; the inescapable struggle and loneliness and pain that
remind us that we are less than God after all, that you have made
us with hard limits, limits to our strength, our knowledge, our days.
Facing those limits, Lord, grant us grace to live to the limit of
being fully alive, irrepressibly alive, of experiencing every fragile,
miraculous, beautiful ounce of human being.

O God, turn your Spirit loose now and us with it, that we may go to where the silence is, and stand together there with folk with Aids, and those affected by it; to face with you the utter mystery of questions without answers, pain without balm, sorrow without comfort, and fears without relief. Facing the mystery, Lord, grant us grace to wrestle with it until we name the fears and force them to set us free, to wrestle with it until the pain teaches us and we befriend it, until the silence subdues us and we are healed by it.

O God, turn your Spirit loose now and us with it, that we may go to where the darkness is, and stand together there with folk with Aids, and those affected by it; to face with you the terrible uncertainty of tomorrow, of what will happen, what might happen, what could happen to us, to our friends, to our jobs, to our relationships, to our world. Facing the uncertainty, Lord, grant us the grace to look at it directly and openly, to laugh at it with faith in the promise that nothing can separate us from your love. And so, despite the dark uncertainty of tomorrow, in the light of our todays, we move on and pray on, held in the palm of your hand.

Go forth in peace. Be still within yourself and know that the trail is beautiful. Walk in beauty and harmony with God and all people. Amen.

(Prayers from the Southwark Cathedral service)

HYMN 141

Guide me, O thou great Jehovah

Beginnings

In 1993 a terrorist act devastated the City of London's oldest and smallest church, St Ethelburga's. The London *Evening Standard* newspaper reported on plans to rejuvenate the site both as a modern monument and as a Christian witness to visitors and passers-by. It headlined its coverage 'A Resurrection in Glass'. The word 'resurrection' was also used to describe the rebuilding of Coventry Cathedral, after much of it was destroyed by German bombing on the fateful night of 14 November 1940. By the next morning there were already signs of new life as the task began of clearing away the mass of rubble, and plans were laid for a new beginning.

Cross and Resurrection are born twins in the Christian faith; nothing can separate one from the other. The faith speaks of innovating intervention in what sometimes seems an ever-rising spiral of evil. Love and creativeness are operative words. Out of death there comes resurrection; from the old the new dawns. The cross is the sign of the collision between the Kingdom of God and the kingdoms of this world. The faith radiates the sense of becoming, for while it takes the dark side of human nature seriously, it nonetheless stresses transformation. It refuses to accept the relentless working out of fate as in a Greek tragedy, for the demonic chain of events has been radically broken.

HYMN 392

New every morning is the love

READING

Ephesians 2.13–20

But now in Christ Jesus you who once were far off have been brought near by the blood of Christ. For he is our peace; in his flesh he has made both groups into one and has broken down the dividing wall, that is, the hostility between us. He has abolished the law with its commandments and ordinances, so that he might create in himself one new humanity in place of the two, thus making peace, and might reconcile both groups to God in one body through the cross, thus putting to death that hostility through it. So he came and proclaimed peace to you who were far off and peace to those who were near; for through him both of us have access in one Spirit to the Father. So then you are no longer strangers and aliens, but you are citizens with the saints and also members of the household of God, built upon the foundation of the apostles and prophets, with Christ Jesus himself as the cornerstone.

PRAYERS

We affirm life.

Jesus Christ, out of love for this world, gives his life.

Because of Christ we affirm life.

Stale repetition, brutality, impersonality, alienation have no place.

Because of Christ we affirm life.

The dehumanizers, the destructionists, the demonic and satanic, will be scattered.

Because of Christ we affirm life.

Terror, despair, demonry, mind-rape, chains, and scourges shall be denied.

Because of Christ we affirm life.

Lord, let us know by our own experience and our willingness to risk life that you are there before us. Enable us to rebuild on the ruins, to re-create what has been destroyed, to restore what has been damaged. Imprint deeply upon our hearts that we must not be negligent nor give way to despair. Teach us to trust you for life and death, to take you for our All in All. Amen.

HYMN 8

Great is thy faithfulness, O God my Father

Books, Words, and Authors

They said the 'read and printed word' would die. The visual forms of film, video, and television would conquer all. It has not been so.

Admittedly, the 'read and printed word' no longer enjoys its former exalted state but book publishing, even if a hazardous business, remains a major activity, and bookshops and book departments within major multiple business concerns are still prominent in the overall retail activity of any reasonable size shopping area.

In most countries the book remains a special item—it is sometimes free from various taxes that can be added to a stated purchase price. The book still possesses power and an ability to shape and form opinion, and this is starkly noticed by the continuing existence of title censorship that operates in countries where free speech is severely curtailed.

Books means business, and for publishing houses and shareholders alike, there is a desire to show an operating profit, whereas most authors, and the majority of those who purchase books, remain oblivious to the business world's machinations. For the reader, what matters most is the ability of a writer to make us fall in love with words. We will embark on an adventure with an author because that person exudes a flavour and scent that attracts us. At the end of reading a good book we should be able to feel that 'Yes, life is worth living'.

A good writer, within the arduous task of first writing, then assembling a book, has invested a massive amount in that work. He or she will have spent hours pursuing perfection, searching for the right word, and developing plot and character. Finally, the author submits the whole work to the critical eye of a publisher.

A few writers receive national acclaim for many countries have yearly book awards. In Britain, amongst the best known are the Booker Prize (available to all writers), and the Orange Prize for Fiction (open to women). Frequently there is considerable disagreement among those who judge as to which writer and title should win, but overall media and public interest keep the book to the fore, and ensure the book will not die.

Christian, Jewish, and Islamic faiths are among the world

religions with a holy book and they keep their scripture alive by having it read in public during their time of worship.

HYMN 255 v4 , 8

Think of a world

READING

Luke 4.16–20a

When he [Jesus] came to Nazareth, where he had been brought up, he went to the synagogue on the sabbath day, as was his custom. He stood up to read, and the scroll of the prophet Isaiah was given to him. He unrolled the scroll and found the place where it was written: 'The Spirit of the Lord is upon me, because he has anointed me to bring good news to the poor. He has sent me to proclaim release to the captives and recovery of sight to the blind, to let the oppressed go free, to proclaim the year of the Lord's favour.' And he rolled up the scroll, gave it back to the attendant, and sat down.

PRAYER

We praise you, God of the Word, for writers and authors, for editors and publishers, printers, and booksellers, and for all who believe in words. We praise you for the gift of words, the beauty of words, the power of words to delight, excite, challenge, change, and feed.

God of the Word,
With words you draw us away from the earth;
With words you can help us to find meaning in the seemingly humdrum;
With words you can lead us into the great search for life and living;
With words you can enable us to reach into worlds that expand our imagination;
With words you uplift and honour our existence.
With the Word, you revealed yourself so that all can realize they are your sons and daughters in Christ.
May your name be praised and known by all.

HYMN 165

Spirit of God, unseen as the wind

Broadcasting

R ecent years have seen major growth in the number of radio stations and television channels. Many people have become uneasy about the kind of programmes some of them transmit. Various bodies have been set up to oversee the content and nature of broadcasting. Some are statutory bodies, others are voluntary groups who have taken on the responsibility of monitoring broadcasts. The best-known critic in the United Kingdom has been Mary Whitehouse who has often railed against what she sees as declining standards, not in terms of professional expertise, but in the type of programme commissioned and the content that has ensued.

One of Britain's major TV critics has said that in current television output every aspect of life is reduced to a metaphorical sound-bite: a punch in the face. She speaks of an increased level of violence and asks, 'Where in the mainstream is the spiritually uplifting stuff, the material with a moral message or dealing with life's big issues, like love and mortality?' She also poses the question, 'whether TV does enough to provide the emotional nourishment to help us through tragedy, and enable us to grow up as human beings when faced with the many problems and predicaments that confront us throughout life'.

The word 'broadcasting' originally meant the scattering of seed. Now that it refers more widely to the dissemination of ideas, images, and words, the debate is whether this should be a controlled or a free activity. Milton said of Truth: 'Let her and Falsehood grapple. Whoever knew Truth put to the worse in a free and open encounter?' Many would see as the two important words in such a maxim, 'free' and 'open'. The intent of those twin ideas has to be safeguarded in a truly democratic society.

READING

John 1.1–5

In the beginning was the Word, and the Word was with God, and the Word was God. He was in the beginning with God. All things came into being through him, and without him not one thing came into being. What has come into being in him was life, and the life was the light of all people. The light shines in the darkness and the darkness did not overcome it.

HYMN 177

Thou whose almighty word

PRAYERS

A prayer for the broadcasters
Word of God, inspire us.
Word of God, inspire us.
Despite the light of the Word, we scramble in the dark for relevant, life-giving, and life-sustaining thoughts.
Challenge our self-satisfactions and our easy securities, our neat presuppositions and systems;
Word of God, inspire us.
Stimulate our minds and creative spirits to rise above the obvious and mundane.
Teach us to respect those for whom we broadcast, write, schedule programmes, make budgets;
Word of God, inspire us.
May we ever hunt down the multi-coloured vision of creativity and the sounds of excellence.
So may we proclaim your name in many guises and feed your children with nourishing food;
Word of God, inspire us.

We pray, O God, for all who speak where many listen, perform what many see, or write what many read. We thank you for their ability to inform, to educate, or to entertain others. Help them to use their talents responsibly so that through their gifts the lives of many may be enriched. May the seeds of truth, of knowledge, and of laughter which they disseminate bring a rich harvest, bearing fruits that honour your name. Amen.

Philippians 4.8

Finally, beloved, whatever is true, whatever is honourable, whatever is just, whatever is pure, whatever is pleasing, whatever is commendable, if there is any excellence and if there is anything worthy of praise, think about these things.

HYMN 163

Gift of Christ from God our Father

Budget Day

There can be little doubt which subject is uppermost in people's minds on this day—money. Almost everyone seems to be working out what the budget will mean for their pocket and how much better or worse off they will be. There is nothing new in all this. Even in the time of Jesus, taxes caused trouble and people were always arguing about why they had to pay them. As we shall see later, Jesus had his say on the subject. But he also reminded people that not everything worthwhile costs money. Indeed, the best things in life are the free gifts of God—the gifts of that love which surrounds us from the day we are born until the day we die. As Joseph Addison the poet puts it, 'Ten thousand thousand precious gifts my daily thanks employ', and he goes on with wonderful exaggeration to say, 'Even eternity's too short to utter all God's praise'. So let us praise God for all his mercies.

HYMN 227
God of mercy, God of grace

THANKSGIVING

Let us thank God for all the gifts we enjoy freely and that we
    value more than anything money can buy:
God, like a good father and mother, you know how to give good
    gifts to your children.
We thank you for those that are on free offer:
for the gift of life itself, renewed moment by moment;
Thanks be to God;
for the air filling our lungs and the blood pulsing through our
    veins;
Thanks be to God;
for the colour and variety of the scenery around us;
Thanks be to God;
for the love which supports us through all the days of our life;
Thanks be to God;
Above all we thank you for the free offer of grace in the
    forgiveness of our sins through the cross of Christ;
Thanks be to God.

Nothing that money can buy could meet our needs as you have met them through your love for us. Yet you know that we do have need of money, to buy our material necessities, to cater for the need of others, to provide for our life together in community. May we earn it honestly, save it prudently, and spend it wisely, to the glory of your name. Amen.

READING

Jesus recognized that money is important and he spoke often of the need for wisdom in the use of it. So he was inevitably drawn into the debate about taxes, especially during the days when his enemies were trying to trap him. Matthew, himself probably once a tax collector, records the story.

Matthew 22.15–22

Then the Pharisees went and plotted to entrap him in what he said. So they sent their disciples to him, along with the Herodians, saying, 'Teacher, we know that you are sincere, and teach the way of God in accordance with truth, and show deference to no one; for you do not regard people with partiality. Tell us, then, what you think. Is it lawful to pay taxes to the emperor, or not?' But Jesus, aware of their malice, said, 'Why are you putting me to the test, you hypocrites? Show me the coin used for the tax.' And they brought him a denarius. Then he said to them, 'Whose head is this, and whose title?' They answered, 'The emperor's.' Then he said to them, 'Give therefore to the emperor the things that are the emperor's, and to God the things that are God's.' When they heard this, they were amazed; and they left him and went away.

PRAYERS

Eternal God, in whose image we are made,
You have impressed the likeness of your Son upon us.
We ask you that we may be more like him in the way we spend
    our lives,
That we may reflect his grace in all our human contacts,
And value the things he valued, the treasures of your Kingdom.
    Amen.

Lord God, we pray for those whose image is imprinted upon the
  currency of our daily lives;
for our Queen and all in authority under her;
for those who serve in Parliament and in the local councils of our
  land;
for those who buy and sell, who transact investments and
  negotiate loans;
that in all the affairs of our economy the concern may be for the
  common good and the welfare of this land and of all nations,
  that your will may be done on earth as it is in heaven. Amen.

Merciful God, we pray for those who have no money and no work,
and who must depend upon the provision of welfare or the gifts of
charity. Grant to those who administer benefit the resources they
need to relieve distress, and give to us all such generous hearts that
we may be willing to share with others the bounty you bestow upon
us, for your name's sake, Amen.

O God who has bound us together in this bundle of life, give us
grace to understand how our lives depend upon the courage, the
industry and the integrity of others, that we may be mindful of
their needs, grateful for their faithfulness, and faithful in our
responsibilities to them, through Jesus Christ our Lord. Amen.
                                    (Reinhold Niebuhr, *OBP* 201)

Lord, grant us wisdom to know what things to value, what riches to
disdain and what reward to give, for your name's sake. Amen.

HYMN 222
For the beauty of the earth

Business

The newspaper article was headed, 'Caring, sharing and whole-foods: that's what life is about at Daily Bread'. A not uninspired guess would deduce it was an article about a Christian Co-operative. Several years ago there was an article in the business section of a Sunday newspaper centring on Community Wholefoods and its director, a Christian, Tim Powell. Powell had begun his company from a squat, with five friends. Powell, as with manager Andrew Hibbert, the founder of Wholefoods, said his business was based upon biblical ethics and guidelines. Apart from particular business matters, both companies have daily worship and prayer, with Community Wholefoods giving 10 per cent of its profits to charity, following an Old Testament precept. Both groups are environmentally concerned, with Powell stressing how 'we need to confess our guilt about what we've done to the environment'. Andrew Hibbert says, 'The sharing of food is a Christian thing to do; the Last Supper is an example of how to share good simple food together. Wholefoods are basic foods'. As the writer of the feature revolving around the Daily Bread Co-operative remarks, shopping and spirituality are two words that hardly trip off the tongue together. But of course there have been, and there remain, some huge companies that have had a Christian base to their dealings in the market-place. While some people suggest that business and Christian ethics do not mix, others disagree, and have set about proving their point.

HYMN 396

For the fruits of his creation

READING

John 6.4–14

Now the Passover, the festival of the Jews, was near. When he looked up and saw a large crowd coming towards him, Jesus said to Philip, 'Where are we to buy bread for these people to eat?' He said this to test him, for he himself knew what he was going to do. Philip answered him, 'Six months' wages would not buy enough bread for each of them to get a little.' One of his disciples, Andrew, Simon Peter's brother, said to him, 'There is a boy here who has five barley loaves and two fish. But what are they among so many people?' Jesus said, 'Make the people sit down.' Now there was a great deal of grass in the place; so they sat down, about five thousand in all. Then Jesus took the loaves, and when he had given thanks, he distributed them to those who were seated; so also the fish, as much as they wanted. When they were satisfied, he told his disciples, 'Gather up the fragments left over, so that nothing may be lost.' So they gathered them up, and from the fragments of the five barley loaves, left by those who had eaten, they filled twelve baskets. When the people saw the sign he had done, they began to say, 'This is indeed the prophet who is to come into the world.'

PRAYER

Jesus said the Kingdom of God is in us, is in you, is in all. The Kingdom is like a seed, already put in the soil.
May we always have a grateful heart, may we be cleansed from guilt and purified from sin.
We bring before the Lord business concerns, great and small, especially [name] in our neighbourhood, those who work there, those who plan and execute policies. May decisions be made with a social conscience and an awareness of people's needs. May decisions reflect fair conditions of work and just payment for services and materials.
Lord, hear this prayer.

We pray for [name ... a business event such as the collapse of a firm or unemployment notices given by a business concern ...].
We pray for those known to us who in their particular circumstances are trying to see where the Christian ethic and the business ethic might agree [name ...].

Father,
You are present in every moment of human experience—
grant to us all the strength to oppose unjust systems,
corrupt, exploitative business concerns, and illegal work practices.
Lord, hear our prayer.

HYMN 168

There's a spirit in the air

Carers

E lton John is a world-acclaimed popular music artist. It took him nearly twenty years before he had his first solo British number one single, but in 1990 he triumphed with *Healing Hands.*

Royalties from the single went to help those suffering from Aids. Aids is a fatal affliction that has affected many people in show business. In dealing with the horrific nature of this illness to the sufferer, the care and concern from medical carers is unsurpassed, but this can often be said when the medical prognosis is terminal. Doubtless there are poor doctors, inefficient nurses, and bad administrative centres in the medical service; yet it would seem that it is an area where there is enormous dedication and concern alongside healing and caring skills.

While illness is of pertinent concern to those who fall under the generalized description of 'medical staff', it seems insufficient to leave matters there. Much positive action for the sufferer can come from the so-called unqualified. On one occasion the *Methodist Recorder* printed a letter from someone who was single, a widow for sixteen years, with no close family to support her. Suddenly she found herself in hospital for a major operation. The hospital was seventeen miles from where she lived. But, speaking of her church, and others with whom she was familiar, she wrote:

I had many visitors. I was flooded with cards and letters, including a card signed by the Sunday School children, and another from a residential home. There were flowers, presents, attention to my personal needs, washing done and beautifully ironed, the loan of a radio, constant phone enquiries as well as plans in hand to give help and support on my return home. All this—for me! Not a celebrity like Viscount Tonypandy. Incidentally his story has been a source of inspiration and encouragement to me. Most important of all was the assurance given in person or by written word that prayers were continually made on my behalf.

The litany of carers could be endless for there are the unsung thousands of partners, daughters, sons, sisters, brothers, friends, who look after the sick and the ever-increasing number of people with senile dementia, often without any back-up, most of whom can rarely take any holiday.

For many people, medical and nursing hands are supplemented

by general hands, praying hands—a powerful cocktail of science and human endeavour, of accepting, loving, comforting, embracing, and caring.

HYMN 370

Christ's is the world in which we move

READING

Luke 10.2–6; 8–9

He said to them, 'The harvest is plentiful, but the labourers are few; therefore ask the Lord of the harvest to send out labourers into his harvest. Go on your way. See, I am sending you out like lambs into the midst of wolves. Carry no purse, no bag, no sandals; and greet no one on the road. Whatever house you enter, first say, "Peace to this house!" And if anyone is there who shares in peace, your peace will rest on that person; but if not, it will return to you . . . Whenever you enter a town and its people welcome you, eat what is set before you; cure the sick who are there, and say to them, "The kingdom of God has come near to you."'

PRAYER

Life is being where you have to be.
So we pray, dear God, for those who dedicate their skills to care
    for and heal the less fortunate—
Those who know that life is being concerned for people.

May all of us support carers with our prayers,
May all of us support healers with various forms of positive
    commitment.

Take time to be aware—
it is the opportunity to help others.
Take time to love and be loved—
it is God's greatest gift.

The living, moving Spirit of God
calls us to care.

HYMN 355

A new commandment

Celebrating Success

When the world-renowned cellist Tortelier celebrated his seventy-fifth birthday, friends came to greet him from all over the world, and to congratulate him on his successful career in the world of music. Among them was his fellow cellist, Rostropovich. Someone asked these two great musicians whether they ever felt they were competing with one another. Tortelier replied, 'No, because we are only servants to the great masters of music. When we play Bach we are both humbled.' When we come into the presence of God, we too are humbled, however great our achievements might be. So we begin our worship today by acknowledging the greatness of the Creator. O Lord my God, how great Thou art.

HYMN 13

How great Thou art

PRAYERS

Lord God, whose greatness has been revealed to us not only through the majesty of your creation but also through the humility of your Son, help us to lay aside all selfish pride in our success and all arrogant boasting, and to measure our lives not by our achievements but by his example. May we lay our success at your feet so that you might show us how it can be used in the service of others, for the sake of Jesus Christ our Lord. Amen.

At this point, announce the names of those whose success is being celebrated and acknowledge their achievement with applause.

Lord we rejoice with all those who receive the reward of success for their hard work and effort. May this achievement mark the way to yet further progress, so that they may be fully equipped to serve you and their fellows to the best of their ability, always pressing on to the goal of their high calling. Amen.

God, we lay at your feet whatever success we have achieved. We thank you for all those whose encouragement, instruction, and support have helped us on our way. We pray that we may press on to the next target you set before us, always seeking to be the best we can be for your sake and for the sake of those who love us and celebrate our success with us. Amen.

RESPONSE
Halle- Halle- Halle- luja (Caribbean) (*WE* 76)

READING
It is hard to be truly humble, not just about our own successes but particularly about the achievements of the people we love. We want others to realize how successful they are, and so we seek high honour for them. Mothers are particularly prone to this kind of boasting, so we can understand the motive behind the special request made to Jesus by the mother of two of his disciples, James and John. We read about it in Matthew's Gospel, chapter 20, beginning to read at verse 20.

Then the mother of the sons of Zebedee came to him with her sons, and kneeling before him, she asked a favour of him. And he said to her, 'What do you want?' She said to him, 'Declare that these two sons of mine will sit, one at your right hand and one at your left, in your kingdom.' But Jesus answered, 'You do not know what you are asking. Are you able to drink the cup that I am about to drink?' They said to him, 'We are able.' He said to them, 'You will indeed drink my cup, but to sit at my right and at my left, this is not mine to grant, but it is for those for whom it has been prepared by my Father.'
    When the ten heard it, they were angry with the two brothers. But Jesus called them to him and said, 'You know that the rulers of the Gentiles lord it over them, and their great ones are tyrants over them. It will not be so among you; but whoever wishes to be great among you must be your servant, and whoever wishes to be first among you must be your slave; just as the Son of Man came not to be served but to serve, and to give his life a ransom for many.'

PRAYERS
Lord Jesus Christ, in all the fullness of your power most gentle, in

your exceeding greatness most humble, bestow your mind and spirit upon us, who have nothing of which to boast; that clothed in true humility, we may be exalted to true greatness, for the glory of your name. Amen.

(Adapted from the Primer of 1559 *NEM* p. 18)

God of all hope, we pray for those we love and for whom we are ambitious. Help us not to push them too far nor demand too much of them. Enable us to rejoice in the flowering of their talents be they great or small, but help us above all to enable them to find their true vocation, not in seeking success but in serving others for your sake. Amen.

Let us pray particularly for those who, having achieved success in their own lives, have dedicated themselves and their skills to the service of others. We think of those many aid workers overseas, who are sharing their talents with people less fortunate than themselves and who in doing so share the heartbreak of the people they have gone to serve. May they find the rest that is promised to those who are heavy laden, through Jesus Christ our Lord.

For all who this day will serve us in any way, great or small, thanks be to God.
On all the service we can give this day to others, great or small, we ask God's blessing. Amen.
So send us out from here, God, as well equipped as we can be to serve a world in need.

HYMN 376
Brother, let me be your servant

Charity Appeals

Flag days, special weeks, television appeals, and pop events remind us continually that there is 'need' either in one's country, or more often than not, where there is famine or tragic human suffering resulting from political and social unrest.

Even a brief look at the registered listing of charities reveals an enormous number of organizations and groups bidding either for an individual's conscious commitment to give away a percentage of income or for what might be called their 'loose change'. Inevitably, it is the larger charities that can claim most attention, and who devote major sums of money from their giving to raise infinitely more. They organize promotional and advertising campaigns and engage staff to direct their appeals. It is an invidious task to name those with the highest profile, and even more difficult to evaluate which can claim the most need.

In British television terms, one of the most successful events in terms of funds raised is the yearly Comic Relief that engages popular entertainers. Monies raised are given to charities submitting their claims, but even here smaller groups appear to be gently nudged out of the way, or at the very least they find it hard to substantiate their claim.

In pop lore, the most publicized global event was on 13 July 1985 when Live Aid brought together a billion people. Thanks to the advantage of the modern miracle of electronic communication, a virtual global juke box was available to the world community. Two concerts called Live Aid were relayed from London and Philadelphia. The aim was to raise money for famine relief in Africa.

HYMN 381

Jesu, Jesu, fill us with your love.

READING

2 Corinthians 9.5–12

So I thought it necessary to urge the brothers to go on ahead to you, and arrange in advance for this bountiful gift that you have promised, so that it may be ready as a voluntary gift and not as an extortion. The point is this: the one who sows sparingly will also reap sparingly, and the one who sows bountifully will also reap bountifully. Each of you must give as you have made up your mind, not reluctantly or under compulsion, for God loves a cheerful giver. And God is able to provide you with every blessing in abundance, so that by always having enough of everything, you may share abundantly in every good work. As it is written, 'He scatters abroad, he gives to the poor; his righteousness endures for ever.' He who supplies seed to the sower and bread for food will supply and multiply your seed for sowing and increase the harvest of your righteousness.

PRAYER

Lord, you have given us so much;
And we are not always grateful.
You feed us with food and water. You give us love. You so
   loved us that you gave us your only Son, who died for us on
   the cross;
And we are not always grateful.
In you, we are all sons and daughters through faith;
And we are not always grateful.
We bring before you the many troubled areas of the world
   [name].
We lay before you the suffering, pain and misery, and famine.
May we have a desire for justice and goodness.
May we not turn a blind eye to the evils and failures of political
   and social systems that cause untold suffering and need.

We pray for people and situations close to us
   [name].
We bring before you the work of many organizations whose task
   rests in alleviating need.
We especially pray for [name] and for their workers [name].

Who is Christ but the man who came to help?
**In the light of that statement, may we re-examine our life
   priorities.**

HYMN 384

Sent by the Lord am I

Children as Victims of Violence

There's an agony that tugs at the heart when we hear of children becoming the victims of violent crime or accident, whether it be here in our own country or overseas. When a crime is committed against a child in our own land, the whole nation is stunned by the news. And every day, in lands overseas, thousands of children die through violence or land mines or the effects of war. It's an agony that moved Jesus himself to anger, as he pronounced his severest judgement on anyone who put a stumbling-block in the way of a little child. His words are recorded in St Matthew's gospel, chapter 18.

READING

At that time the disciples came to Jesus and asked, 'Who is the greatest in the kingdom of heaven?' He called a child, whom he put among them, and said, 'Truly I tell you, unless you change and become like children, you will never enter the kingdom of heaven. Whoever becomes humble like this child is the greatest in the kingdom of heaven. Whoever welcomes one such child in my name welcomes me.

'If any of you put a stumbling-block before one of these little ones who believe in me, it would be better for you if a great millstone were fastened around your neck and you were drowned in the depth of the sea. Woe to the world because of stumbling-blocks! Occasions for stumbling are bound to come, but woe to the one by whom the stumbling-block comes! . . .

'Take care that you do not despise one of these little ones; for, I tell you, in heaven their angels continually see the face of my Father in heaven.'

HYMN 155

Loving shepherd of thy sheep

PRAYERS BY CHILDREN (read if possible by children)

Dear God, it is good to know that you are always around. Thank you. That's all.

And now dear God, what can I do for you?

Lord, I just don't know what to say when I'm asked to make a
  prayer. It is like being asked to breathe.

God, I love you because they tell me you love me. Please go on
  loving me even when I don't deserve it.

Dear God, I don't ever feel alone since I found out about you.

Lord, give us a new world in which we can be happy, in which
  we can have friends and work together for a good future. A
  world in which there will not be any cruel people who seek to
  destroy us in so many ways. Amen.

Lord, may the trust of such children never be betrayed. Amen.

CHILDREN'S SONG 273

Jesus bids us shine

PRAYERS

God, our Parent, we pray for all parents who are suffering the loss
of a child through a criminal act or accident. We ask that your
comfort may be given to those who mourn, your strength to those
who are angry, your mercy to those who feel remorse; bring to true
penitence those who are to blame for the suffering of children and
grant your wisdom to those who must pass judgement on them.

We entrust the children we have lost into your safe keeping,

May we never cause your little ones to stumble.

Lover of all children, you share the sense of shock and shame
which overwhelms us when we hear of a child we know becoming a
victim of sudden violence. May it make us more sensitive to that
grief which must constantly be in your heart when moment by
moment, day by day, year by year, life is snatched away from your
little ones through the violence of the world we live in. Forgive us
for the greed that causes their hunger, the arms and landmines that
do them injury, the injustice that causes their neglect. Bring us in
our privileged societies to a greater awareness of the needs of the
world's children.

We entrust all children who suffer into your safe keeping,

May we never cause your little ones to stumble.

Bless all those who come to the aid of children, both at times of
sudden peril and through all the days of their need. Hasten the day

when the nations of the world shall recognize the rights of all children to grow up in safety, peace, and fulfilment of all their gifts.

We entrust the children of the world into your safe keeping,

May we never cause your little ones to stumble.

Finally, let us pray particularly for the children we love—our own, or our grandchildren, or godchildren, the children of our friends and neighbours. In our mind's eye let us see them in that group gathered around Jesus for his blessing. May the Lord bless them and keep them. May the Lord make his face to shine upon them and be gracious unto them. May the Lord lift up the light of his countenance upon them and give them peace.

HYMN 293

God who made the earth

Child Slavery

Children in some parts of the world are being abducted, indoctrinated, and even given military training where they have been kidnapped by state agencies. Families have become so fearful that many will not allow their children out unsupervised. In areas where the sale of child labourers is an approved custom, prices vary according to the type of child, with fully grown girls fetching the highest price as future brides.

No form of slavery, let alone one that involves children, finds acceptance in Christian thought. Such a concept flies against a faith that places emphasis upon the uniqueness and equal value of each person. No one can own us but God. He it is who gives us true identity. That is the essence of Scripture teaching. Not least, it is found in the profound words that open the Gospel of John, where humankind is reminded of its daughtership and sonship. It is a message that flies defiantly against those who would imprison and abuse others.

HYMN 266

By the Babylonian rivers

READINGS

John 1.10–13

He was in the world, and the world came into being through him; yet the world did not know him. He came to what was his own, and his own people did not accept him. But to all who received him, who believed in his name, he gave power to become children of God, who were born, not of blood or of the will of the flesh or of the will of man, but of God.

Luke 4.18–19

'The Spirit of the Lord is upon me, because he has anointed me to bring good news to the poor. He has sent me to proclaim release to the captives and recovery of sight to the blind, to let the oppressed go free, to proclaim the year of the Lord's favour.'

PRAYER

Let us pray
for those in despair about their own lives,
for young—often very young—people,
for those who are given no value other than their price,
for those who are abused and mistreated,
for those suffering from their ill-treatment at the hands of the
powerful;
The Lord hears our prayer and gives us hope.

Let us pray
for adult men and women who are uncaring,
for those with hearts of stone,
for those cruel people who support oppression,
for regimes who exploit the vulnerable and powerless,
for systems that tolerate the expenditure of young life,
The Lord hears our prayer and gives us hope.

Give us, O Lord, churches and people
that will not merely 'comfort the afflicted' but 'afflict the
comfortable';
that will not only love but judge in love;
that will not pursue peace by abdicating justice;
that will not be silent with the silenced;
that will not be deaf to the cries of the suffering.

**Teach us, O Lord, what it means to take up the cross and follow
you.**
Teach us, O Lord, what it is to be the people of our prayers.

HYMN 328

Go forth and tell!

City

According to a Methodist, the Reverend John Kennedy, writing in the *Independent* newspaper's weekly feature 'Faith and Reason', one of the most exciting ventures of the Church of England in the latter part of the twentieth century rests in its 1983 project and publication *Faith in the City*. In this work it challenged Church and Nation to respond to the needs of the poor. Kennedy saw the Church speaking out 'where it mattered'.

There are more than a thousand references to cities in the Bible but the city in modern terms usually contains at least one million people, often many more, and with citizens living in close proximity. It is hardly the simple scenario familiar to biblical writers. The interests of the Hebrews were largely pastoral. Some theologians have adored the large modern and densely populated city; none more so, in the 1960s, than Harvey Cox, an American who saw the city offering freedom for people to live their lives the way they wished, generally free from tribal boundaries, and small-town prejudices and observations. Others have seen quite the opposite, noting the innate loneliness of many who live in cities, and the abject misery often experienced by those without work, who in recent times have become noticeable as they squat in their cardboard boxes in the shop doorways of many cities. Yet few would deny that a modern city possesses energy and vitality, for there is always the paradox that creativity can stem from want and hunger. Many a musician, struggling actor, desperate painter, and angry poet can testify to this, and equally speak of their lack of creativity once they have known the fat of the land.

HYMN 386

Judge eternal, throned in splendour

READING

Matthew 23.37–9

'Jerusalem, Jerusalem, the city that kills the prophets and stones those who are sent to it! How often have I desired to gather your children together as a hen gathers her brood under her wings, and you were not willing! See, your house is left to you, desolate. For I tell you, you will not see me again until you say, "Blessed is the one who comes in the name of the Lord."'

PRAYERS

When will you save the people?
O God of mercy, when?
Lord, we offer you our cities;
we offer you the many cultures;
we bring before you for blessing
creative and energizing opportunities.
We name ... and ... and ...
Lord hear our prayer.
Lord, we bring before you our cities;
we lay before you the many cultures;
we bring before you for blessing
the pain of people lost,
those abused for skin colour.
Lord, hear our prayer.
Jesus, your name means healing;
Jesus, have pity on us.
Jesus, you touch those who need affirming;
Jesus, stop by for us.
Jesus, you give hope where there is none;
Jesus, give us rage and anger to right wrongs.

HYMN 332

Jesus Christ is waiting

Courage Awards

Angela was 7 when she suffered major injury. Run over by a car, she lost her left ear and had various fractures of the leg. It was said she would never walk again, yet in less than a month she took her first steps. Robbie, aged 4, fell into a scalding bath and for a third of a year slept balanced on his knees and forehead. Angela, with Robbie and numerous other young people possessed of extraordinary resilience and bravery have been justly recognized in the yearly Children of Courage awards.

Children can remind us that self-belief is essential to any person's well-being, and by their youth can make the point all the more clearly. Once someone loses the desire 'to be' then there is an uphill task for anyone who cares enough for that person to bring about a change of mind. Physical injury and illness, where the prognosis may be bad, can produce a regressive retreat into self-pity, acute estrangement, and lack of will. In some instances it is hardly surprising if this occurs.

Yet at the same time, against all odds, there are those who triumph against all adversity, and who, at least, refuse to accept their state. The courage of many suffering people often shames the well, and at very least asks them to consider if they are intelligently making use of their own gift of good health. For those who suffer, it seems as though all fate is arraigned against them, and if there is religious faith it may well seem as though God is absent from their lives. True faith knows of a suffering God, and that through all adversity he is present. In that sense the last verse of the chosen psalm rings true.

HYMN 224

Give thanks with a grateful heart

READING

Psalm 13

How long, O Lord? Will you forget me for ever?
How long will you hide your face from me?

How long must I bear pain in my soul,
and have sorrow in my heart all day long?
How long shall my enemy be exalted over me?
Consider and answer me, O Lord my God!
Give light to my eyes, or I will sleep the sleep of death,
and my enemy will say, 'I have prevailed';
my foes will rejoice because I am shaken.
But I trusted in your steadfast love;
my heart shall rejoice in your salvation.
I will sing to the Lord,
because he has dealt bountifully with me.

PRAYERS

We will praise you, O Lord, whatever happens.
We will know your presence in our distress,
Yet we know how hard it will be to say such sentiments if we
should fall ill.
While we are well, build our faith and trust in you.
Enable us to use our lives so that we seek the truths of existence.
May we learn of the life beyond our mortal bodies.
Let us know that to live is Christ, to die is gain.

Into your care and keeping we commit [names], brave and
courageous in their suffering.
Teach us not to patronize them, but to share a power in their
powerlessness.
Amen.

HYMN 334

Lord, make me a mountain standing tall for you

Creation

'The earth is the Lord's and the fullness thereof', sang the psalmist. For too long, human beings have acted as though the earth belonged to them and have damaged and depleted its resources. Daily, it seems, we hear of new threats to the environment through pollution or waste or destruction. This is more than a problem of keeping a proper ecological balance. 'The earth will not be saved simply because people renounce aerosols or start using cruelty-free cosmetics,' wrote Jonathan Porritt in a recent article in the *Radio Times*. 'But at the individual or lifestyle level, what is the next step? Not just consuming greener products, but consuming less; achieving a higher quality of life by cutting out unnecessary hassle; and spending more time on relationships, on the community, on interaction with the natural world, and even (dare one say it?) on spiritual concerns.'

HYMN 391

Morning has broken

PRAYER

Creator God, whose praises are sung by the birds of the air, and whose beauty is reflected in the flowers of the field, help us to join in that song of praise and to glow with that radiance which is given to those who turn their faces to the sun and bask in your presence. Save us from being so hassled that we have no time to enjoy the beauty of the world around us. And help us in every spare moment to lift up our hearts in thanksgiving for all the provision you have made for us and for all your creatures. So may this time of worship be a time of re-creation for our souls and of reverence for your world.

The poet Gerard Manley Hopkins glorifies God even in the midst of a smudged environment:

> The world is charged with the grandeur of God.
> It will flame out, like shining from shook foil;

It gathers to a greatness, like the ooze of oil
Crushed. Why do men then now not reck his rod?
Generations have trod, have trod, have trod;
   And all is seared with trade; bleared, smeared with toil;
   And wears man's smudge and shares man's smell: the soil
Is bare now, nor can foot feel, being shod.

And, for all this, nature is never spent;
   There lives the dearest freshness deep down things;
And though the last lights off the black West went
   Oh, morning, at the brown brink eastwards, springs—
Because the Holy Ghost over the bent
   World broods with warm breast and with ah! bright wings.

READING

The first book of Genesis, in reverse (with apologies to Colin Morris!)

On the sixth day, Adam and Eve said, 'Now we are in charge. The animals are ours, to use as we will, to experiment with, to slaughter, and to devour,' until the day came when animal disease infected humankind.

And they saw that it was bad.

And on the fifth day Adam and Eve learned to sail the seas and to soar through the air. And they built great warships, and hid submarines in the depths of the ocean, and they invented powerful bombs and fired rockets into space, until the day came when their enemies attacked them.

And they saw that it was bad.

And on the fourth day Adam and Eve learned to kindle fire and make light. They harnessed electric power and invented combustion engines. And the glare of their lighting hid the light of the stars, and the fumes of their engines polluted the atmosphere.

And they saw that it was bad.

And on the third day Adam and Eve divided up the world God had made into continents and nations. And some were powerful and others were powerless. And the powerful plundered the resources of the powerless until some lands were rich and some were poor.

And they saw that it was bad.

And on the second day Adam and Eve decided to explore the realms beyond their planet. And they soared up into space and said they could not find God there. So they decided they had no need of God. But they could no longer tell light from dark, nor good from evil.

And they saw that it was bad.

And on the first day Adam and Eve began to think of themselves as gods. They unleashed their mighty power so that it hung over the whole world as a threatening mushroom cloud. And they became afraid that they might one day destroy the earth itself.

And they saw that it was bad.

And in the end there was a big bang, as there had been at the beginning. And God said, 'We'll have to start all over again.'

PRAYERS

God, Creator of this universe, you have made all things good.
Forgive us for the ways in which we have spoilt your handiwork.
For the way we have disturbed the delicate balance of our
    natural world;
God, forgive us.
For the way we have polluted its atmosphere by our carelessness
    and waste;
God, forgive us.
For the way we have plundered its resources by our greed and
    neglect;
God, forgive us.

Give us a greater sense of the harmony of your whole creation, a greater reverence for the beauty of the natural world, and a greater generosity in sharing and replenishing the earth's provision, for the sake of all your children. Amen.

A Gaelic Blessing

Deep peace of the running wave to you,
Deep peace of the flowing air to you,
Deep peace of the quiet earth to you,
Deep peace of the shining stars to you,
Deep peace of the Son of Peace to you, forever.

HYMN 1

All creatures of our God and King

Times of Crisis

The Chinese word for 'crisis' can also be translated 'dangerous opportunity'. It is a time for judgement, for reflecting on what has gone wrong in the past, and speculating on what might happen in the future. It presents an opportunity to reassess priorities, to repent of past errors, and to make new decisions. It reminds us of how temporary so many of our plans are, how subject we are to changes in the world around us, and of how much we need to depend for our peace of mind on God's eternal changelessness.

HYMN 357

Father, Lord of all creation

PRAYER

God of the present moment, as we pass through these uncertain times, make us certain of your presence with us and teach us so to live in your presence, that we may abide in your peace all the days of our life. Amen.

(NEM p. 42)

PSALM

I waited patiently for the Lord;
he inclined to me and heard my cry.
He drew me up from the desolate pit;
out of the miry bog;
and set my feet upon a rock
making my steps secure.
He put a new song in my mouth, a song of praise to our God.
Many will see and fear, and put their trust in the Lord.

CHANT

Santo, Santo, Santo—Holy, Holy, Holy (Argentina)   *(WE* 37)

READING

Jesus said 'Peace I leave with you, my peace I give to you. I do not give to you as the world gives. Do not let your hearts be troubled, and do not let them be afraid.' As an illustration of that trust which can give us a right sense of priorities he drew attention to the flowers of the field and the birds of the air who fulfil their God-given role in life with a simple, carefree spontaneity. Matthew chapter 6 beginning at verse 19:

'Do not store up for yourselves treasures on earth, where moth and rust consume and where thieves break in and steal; but store up for yourselves treasures in heaven, where neither moth nor rust consumes and where thieves do not break in and steal. For where your treasure is, there will your heart be also ... Therefore I tell you, do not worry about your life, what you will eat or what you will drink, or about your body, what you will wear. Is not life more than food, and the body more than clothing? Look at the birds of the air; they neither sow nor reap nor gather into barns, and yet your heavenly Father feeds them. Are you not of more value than they? And can any of you by worrying add a single hour to your span of life? And why do you worry about clothing? Consider the lilies of the field, how they grow; they neither toil nor spin, yet I tell you, even Solomon in all his glory was not clothed like one of these. But if God so clothes the grass of the field, which is alive today and tomorrow is thrown into the oven, will he not much more clothe you—you of little faith? Therefore do not worry, saying, "What will we eat?" or "What will we drink?" or "What will we wear?" For it is the Gentiles who strive for all these things; and indeed your heavenly Father knows that you need all these things. But strive first for the kingdom of God and his righteousness, and all these things will be given to you as well. So do not worry about tomorrow, for tomorrow will bring worries of its own. Today's trouble is enough for today.

PRAYER

Because life is uncertain,
But you are unchanging,
We turn to you, God.
Because our plans are in jeopardy,
But your purpose prevails,
We turn to you, God.
Because we fear for the future,

But you teach us to trust,
We turn to you, God.
Because we desire many things
But you meet all our needs,
We turn to you, God.
Because we strive for your kingdom,
But it is close at hand,
We turn to you, God.
Let not our hearts be troubled
But give us your peace.
Amen.

God of love, we cannot count the blessings you have bestowed upon us in the past. So help us to trust you with the future. Guide us in the decisions we have to make. Make your way plain before us and give us the courage to walk in it.

Lord, give us your peace that passes understanding,
And the peace which comes through understanding.
Give us peace in our relationships,
And the peace which comes through reconciliation.
Give us peace in our society,
And the peace which comes through justice.
Give us peace which the world cannot give,
And the peace which the world longs for.
Give us peace in our hearts,
And peace in our homes.
Give us peace when we sleep,
And peace when we rise up to do your will. Amen.

HYMN 319

When we walk with the Lord

Debt

W̶e live in an economy of debt. Personal finances rely increasingly on credit cards, mortgages, and bank loans. International finance has resulted in a debt crisis crippling the poorer nations, whose interest repayments often far outstrip the amount they receive in aid. In biblical times, to be in debt was regarded as a kind of enslavement. So it was decreed that provision must be made at a time of jubilee, that is, every fifty years, for debts to be written off. It was recognized that all property, and particularly all land, ultimately belongs to God and that therefore no human being can demand total possession of it, or use it to exploit others. Our first hymn reminds us of our debt to God for all that we own.

HYMN 368

Son of God, eternal Saviour

PRAYER

Lord you are the giver of life.
In the midst of poverty, we celebrate your promise of plenty.
In the midst of exploitation, we celebrate your promise of justice.
In the midst of greed, we celebrate your promise of generosity.
In the midst of debt, we celebrate the promise of jubilee.
In the midst of despair, we celebrate the promise of hope.
In the midst of disgrace, we celebrate the gospel of grace.

ACCLAMATION

Hallelujah, Hallelujah (Zimbabwe)   (*WE* 61)

READING

In one of the parables told by Jesus the chief character is a man involved in a massive debt. The amount of money involved—the equivalent of two billion pounds in our money—suggests that he was probably a minister of state, handling the financial affairs of a whole nation. But some of the money had gone missing and he seems to have believed that by some rearranging of the finances he might be able to pay it back. In response to the chancellor's pleas for mercy, his creditor dealt with him generously. But none of that generosity was passed on to the much poorer man below him, who owed the chancellor a comparatively trivial sum, equal to about £5. The story is found in Matthew, chapter 18, beginning at verse 23:

'For this reason, the kingdom of heaven may be compared to a king who wished to settle accounts with his slaves. When he began the reckoning, one who owed him ten thousand talents was brought to him; and, as he could not pay, his lord ordered him to be sold, together with his wife and children and all his possessions, and payment to be made. So the slave fell on his knees before him, saying, "Have patience with me, and I will pay you everything." And out of pity for him, the lord of that slave released him and forgave him the debt. But that same slave, as he went out, came upon one of his fellow-slaves who owed him a hundred denarii; and seizing him by the throat he said, "Pay what you owe." Then his fellow-slave fell down and pleaded with him, "Have patience with me, and I will pay you." But he refused; then he went and threw him into prison until he should pay the debt. When his fellow-slaves saw what had happened, they were greatly distressed, and they went and reported to their lord all that had taken place. Then his lord summoned him and said to him, "You wicked slave! I forgave you all that debt because you pleaded with me. Should you not have had mercy on your fellow-slave, as I had mercy on you?" And in anger his lord handed him over to be tortured until he should pay his entire debt. So my heavenly Father will also do to every one of you, if you do not forgive your brother or sister from your heart.'

Notice that in the story the prayer of both men is exactly the same, 'Have patience with me and I will pay you.' The chancellor receives a gracious response; his servant is disgracefully treated. Grace and disgrace are the opposite of one another. Finally, the chancellor himself falls from grace to disgrace. Let us pray now for the grace of God, remembering especially those who receive disgraceful treatment at the hand of their fellows.

PRAYERS

We pray for all who are saddled with heavy burdens of personal debt, for those who are evicted from their homes because they cannot pay their mortgage; for those who have gone bankrupt; for those made redundant.

Lord, be patient with us,

and help us to relieve the burden of debt.

We pray for all who suffer deprivation in countries impoverished by debt, for those who have to cut back their programmes of welfare, health, and education in order to pay off the interest on debts they have incurred, and for all who suffer as a result of those adjustments.

Lord, be patient with us,

and help us to relieve the burden of debt.

We pray for all who seek refuge in more prosperous lands, for those who can find no place to welcome them, and for all who are the present victims of past exploitation.

Lord, be patient with us,

and help us to relieve the burden of debt.

We pray for all communities where compassion is sacrificed to market forces, where the welfare of society is imperilled by economic policies, and where aid is swallowed up by the need to repay debts.

Lord, be patient with us,

and help us to relieve the burden of debt.

We pray that the leaders of the trading nations may have the grace to work out the means whereby rich and poor nations alike can share your bounty.

Lord, be patient with us,

and help us to relieve the burden of debt.

Lord, give us this day our daily bread, and forgive us our debts as we forgive those who are indebted to us. Bring us not to a time of testing, but deliver us from the evil effects of our own actions. For yours is the kingdom, the power, and the glory, now and for evermore. **Amen.**

HYMN 377

For the healing of the nations

Disability

It is difficult to define what is meant by 'disability'. So often the people who are called 'disabled' have abilities far more impressive than those who are considered 'able'. Their greatest disability is most likely to be society's inability to recognize the contribution they have to make to our common life. So we begin our worship today by praising some of the great and famous men and women who are known for their creative gifts rather than for the disability which might have imposed limitations upon them. Our first hymn was written by one of the greatest of English poets, John Milton, who himself was blind.

HYMN 11

Let us, with a gladsome mind

ROLL OF HONOUR

Let us now praise famous men and women who are known in the worlds of the creative arts, of politics, of science, and of scholarship, not for their disabilities but for their achievements: (People could be asked to name any of whom they know. The list could include the following names, to be read out by various voices.)

Ludwig van Beethoven (composer), Gabriel Fauré (composer), Evelyn Glennie (percussionist), Itzhak Perlman (violinist), Cyril Smith (pianist), Jeffrey Tate (conductor), Stevie Wonder (pop star), Henri de Toulouse-Lautrec (painter), Michael Flanders (entertainer), Theodore Roosevelt (statesman), Jack Ashley (politician), David Blunkett (politician), Stephen Hawking (scientist), John Hull (professor of education), Mary Weir (theologian).

For all that these men and women have been able to contribute to our common life, we thank God.

PRAYERS OF TWO PEOPLE WITH DISABILITIES

Paul Leake, who is a probation officer, is blind, and his wife Brenda has multiple sclerosis. They express their faith and their need in the following prayers:

Lord, you love us as we are, with our differences,
whether of physical ability, or of attitude, or of overall character.
You want to bring wholeness to our lives—
to our personalities, to our emotions, to our relationship
to you, to one another, and to our own bodies.
We do not have to pretend with you: we can say it like it is—
we can be angry, be sad, be joyful, be reflective.
You can bring good out of things
that are debilitating, painful, and restrictive.
But the hard thing is when others will not stand alongside
because they are afraid to acknowledge their own weakness.
Teach us to value each other with our differences,
to embrace the opportunities they bring, both for ourselves and
    in others,
and to pray with faith for each other to you,
our maker, healer, and restorer.

(Paul Leake)

Heavenly Father, when I remember that you came to earth as a
    human being,
and experienced the pain, the loss, and the sadness that is
    sometimes ours,
and experienced too the physical disabilities that some of us
    have,
I know that you are with me in my isolation.
Give me faith to believe in your healing power for me,
and help me in the bad times to open myself up to others,
so that they might see your love through me.

(Brenda Leake)

READING

St Paul seems to have suffered from some kind of disability.
Whatever it was, his prayers for deliverance from it seem to have
gone unanswered. But in his disability he discovered a strength that
is made perfect through weakness. The second letter to the
Corinthians, chapter 12, beginning to read at verse 5:

On my own behalf I will not boast, except of my weaknesses. But if I wish to boast, I will not be a fool, for I will be speaking the truth. But I refrain from it, so that no one may think better of me than what is seen in me or heard from me, even considering the exceptional character of the revelations. Therefore, to keep me from being too elated, a thorn was given to me in the flesh, a messenger of Satan to torment me, to keep me from being too elated. Three times I appealed to the Lord about this, that it would leave me, but he said to me, 'My grace is sufficient for you, for power is made perfect in weakness.' So, I will boast all the more gladly of my weaknesses, so that the power of Christ may dwell in me. Therefore I am content with weaknesses, insults, hardships, persecutions, and calamities, for the sake of Christ; for whenever I am weak, then I am strong.

PRAYERS

God of all grace, help us all to recognize our own weakness and to rejoice in the strength of others, particularly those whom we are tempted to regard as weak. Help us to honour your image in those of your servants whose bodies have been damaged or whose abilities are restricted. May we see them as you intended them to be, freed from all impairment and freed from the imprisonment imposed by our prejudice.

Response: **When I am weak, then I am strong.**

Lord, we pray that the life of our society may be so ordered that all may have access to its benefits. Help us to be particularly aware of the needs of those who cannot move about freely, or cannot see, or cannot hear. Show us how best to enable them to enjoy the abundant life which is your will for us all.

Response: **When I am weak, then I am strong.**

Lord, we commend to your care those with special needs, whose minds work slowly and who struggle to learn. We ask your blessing on all who care for them and teach them. Grant to parents and teachers a special measure of patience, and the reward of seeing a response of love.

Response: **When I am weak, then I am strong.**

A prayer of the parents of a child with a disability:

Lord, you have given us this special child to love; give us too a special patience, that we may delight together in simple things, and encourage one another along every small and difficult step of life's journey.

Glory be to God, whose power working in us can do infinitely more than we can ask or imagine. Amen.

HYMN 325

Father, hear the prayer we offer

Disaster in a Community

'Tragedy does not take away love. It increases it. Perhaps we are now more loving people because of our shared grief.' Such was the testimony of the survivor of a sudden disaster that engulfed a whole community. 'God's heart was the first of all our hearts to break,' affirmed a minister of religion, trying to find words of comfort for a congregation plunged into mourning. Words do not come easily at a time of great sorrow. More important are the gestures, the tokens, the symbols of love. Immediately after any disaster, it is through the people who come to the rescue, through the outpouring of speechless sympathy, through the many practical acts of support, that we learn that love remains among us. When we are tempted to ask, 'Where is God at such a time as this?' we can only believe that wherever there is love, there is God.

> And when human hearts are breaking
> Under sorrow's iron rod,
> Then they find that selfsame aching
> Deep within the heart of God

HYMN 5

God is love: let heaven adore him

PRAYER

God of love, we come before you in our numbness. Sudden disaster has silenced our hearts and sapped our souls. We find it difficult to make any sense of what has happened. Our faith is small, but our need is great, and we do not know where else to turn. We come to ask for strength to bear this unexpected anguish. Speak to us words of comfort and let the light of your love so shine through our darkness that we may not be overwhelmed by despair, but may look for the daybreak, when God himself will wipe away all tears from our eyes. Amen.

PSALM

Some verses from Psalm 42 in which the psalmist pours out his grief to God:

As a deer longs for flowing streams, so my soul longs for you, O
   God.
My soul thirsts for God, for the living God. When shall I come and
   behold the face of God?
My tears have been my food day and night, while people say to me
   continually, 'Where is your God?'
These things I remember, as I pour out my soul: how I went with
   the throng, and led them in procession to the house of God,
with glad shouts and songs of thanksgiving,
a multitude keeping festival.
Why are you cast down, O my soul,
and why are you disquieted within me?
Hope in God; for I shall again praise him,
my help and my God.

CHANT (*WE* 81)

Ubi caritas, et amor, ubi caritas, Deus ibi est
Where there is charity and love, there is God.
When disaster struck, help came quickly;
where there is love, there is God.
When the bad news broke, comfort was close at hand;
where there is love, there is God.
When the injured were rescued, skilled care was given;
where there is love, there is God.
When our hearts were breaking, strong arms held us;
where there is love, there is God.
When we poured out our grief, God heard our prayer;
where there is love, there is God.

READING

Romans 8.35–9

Who will separate us from the love of Christ? Will hardship, or
distress, or persecution, or famine, or nakedness, or peril, or
sword? As it is written, 'For your sake, we are being killed all day
long; we are accounted as sheep to be slaughtered.' No, in all these
things we are more than conquerors through him who loved us. For
I am convinced that neither death, nor life, nor angels, nor rulers,
nor things present, nor things to come, nor powers, nor height, nor

depth, nor anything else in all creation, will be able to separate us from the love of God in Christ Jesus our Lord.

PRAYERS

God of all consolation, in your unending love and mercy for us, you turn the darkness of death into the dawn of new life. Show compassion on your people in their sorrow. Be our refuge and strength to lift us from the darkness of this grief to the peace and light of your presence.

We remember before you by name those who have died in this disaster, thanking you for all that their lives meant to us, and commending their souls into your care.

Silence

We pray for the injured and all who care for them, asking that your healing power may be with them.

Silence

We pray for all who must investigate the cause of this tragedy and ask that they may do their work so diligently that future disaster of this kind may be averted.

Silence

We pray for any upon whom blame must fall, that their remorse may lead to repentance and to a resolve to amend their ways.

Silence

We pray for ourselves, that through this sad experience we may learn to value more highly this fragile gift of life and love and to put our faith in an even fuller life beyond.

And may the peace and the love of God bring peace to our hearts this day and in all the days ahead. Amen.

HYMN 286

Be still, my soul

Disgrace

Fortunately errant clergy are few. However, when there is a 'defrocking' the general press considers it most newsworthy. In 1995 Chris Brain, a young priest in Sheffield, particularly known for methods and views with considerable appeal to young people, was disciplined after numerous charges of misbehaviour were levelled against him. The Archdeacon of Sheffield, the Venerable Stephen Lowe, admitted in the London *Evening Standard* that 'He developed a tendency not only to look like a Sunday school picture of Jesus, he began to behave like one, complete with disciples.' Brain's 'home-base team', as he called them, were seemingly far from the rugged New Testament followers; they were 'lycra-clad lovelies'. While Brain's sad saga may prove titillating to many, the wider ramifications concern the use and abuse of power by those who exercise authority, and have control over the lives of others. In numerous areas, people, for one reason or another, have abused their position and status.

HYMN 136

Be thou my guardian and my guide

READING

Philippians 2.3–11

Do nothing from selfish ambition or conceit, but in humility regard others as better than yourselves. Let each of you look not to your own interests, but to the interests of others. Let the same mind be in you that was in Christ Jesus, who, though he was in the form of God, did not regard equality with God as something to be exploited, but emptied himself, taking the form of a slave, being born in human likeness. And being found in human form, he humbled himself and became obedient to the point of death—even death on a cross. Therefore God also highly exalted him and gave him the name that is above every name, so that at the name of Jesus every knee should bend, in heaven and on earth and under the earth, and every tongue should confess that Jesus Christ is Lord, to the glory of God the Father.

PRAYERS

In your open arms,
The love of God shines.

(St Hippolytus, third century)

Blessed are those who know their need of God:
may we hear and know these words as ours.

God, mother and father,
Sow in our souls true love for you and for one another:
may we hear and know these words as ours.
Enable us to understand what it means to be humble:
may we hear and know these words as ours.
Give us the desire to do what you require:
may we hear and know these words as ours.
Help us to know what pain we inflict upon others in pursuance of
  our aims and desires:
may we hear and know these words as ours.
Reveal clearly those jarring passions and desires that speak more
  of us, and our fallen nature, than your will:
may we hear and know these words as ours.
Let us be those who are prepared to walk by forgiveness:
may we hear and know these words as ours.

We plead for your mercy and judgement.
We will allow your love to drive from us all that is unhealthy and
  wrong in our plans.
We welcome the power of those who have none.
We welcome the power of those who are free from taint and wrong.
We welcome the power of those who choose and decide.
We will live for Christ who died,
We will greet his Kingdom with meekness,
We will strive for justice and right,
We will uphold, stand beside, be for, care for the vulnerable,
  whose lives are in the process of early growth.
We will follow Jesus the Servant.

HYMN 331

Jesus calls us! O'er the tumult

Drought

Water is life. It is as physically vital to our well-being as blood. Those of us who live in well-watered lands take it for granted until a brief drought begins to cause alarm. But for the majority of people across the world, the supply of water is a daily preoccupation, and the rains a threat, either because they come too heavily and cause floods, or they fail to come at all and cause a long-lasting drought, reducing the land to desert conditions. Those on whose territory the desert is ever encroaching have no inhibitions about praying for rain. Such prayer is a regular part of their liturgy and a constant reminder of how dependent we are upon God's bounty and upon the regularity of the climate. At harvest time we too remember to be grateful for the rain!

HYMN 401

We plough the fields and scatter

PSALM

> O God, you are my God, I seek you,
> **my soul thirsts for you,**
> my flesh faints for you
> **as in a dry and thirsty land where there is no water.**
> So I have looked upon you in the sanctuary,
> **beholding your power and glory.**
> Because your steadfast love is better than life,
> **my lips will praise you.**
> So I will bless you as long as I live.
> **I will lift up my hands and call on your name.**

ACCLAMATION

Allelulia, Allelulia (Russia)   (*WE* 138)

For the prophets of Israel, the image of water springing up in the desert was a powerful symbol of the refreshment which God's presence would bring to those who had lived long in exile.

READING

Isaiah 35

The wilderness and the dry land shall be glad, the desert shall
rejoice and blossom; like the crocus it shall blossom abundantly,
and rejoice with joy and singing. The glory of Lebanon shall be
given to it, the majesty of Carmel and Sharon. They shall see the
glory of the Lord, the majesty of our God.

Strengthen the weak hands, and make firm the feeble knees. Say
to those who are of a fearful heart, 'Be strong, do not fear! Here is
your God. He will come with vengeance, with terrible recompense.
He will come and save you.' Then the eyes of the blind shall be
opened, and the ears of the deaf unstopped; then the lame shall
leap like a deer, and the tongue of the speechless sing for joy. For
waters shall break forth in the wilderness, and streams in the
desert; the burning sand shall become a pool, and the thirsty
ground springs of water; the haunt of jackals shall become a
swamp, the grass shall become reeds and rushes.

> Jesus said: 'If you knew the gift of God, and who it is who is
> saying to you "Give me a drink", you would have asked him
> and he would have given you living water.'
>
> **Give us that water, that we may never be thirsty.**
>
> Jesus said: 'Those who drink of the water that I will give them
> will never be thirsty.'
>
> **Give us that water, that we may never be thirsty.**
>
> Jesus said: 'The water that I will give will become in them a
> spring of water gushing up to eternal life.'
>
> **Give us that water, that we may never be thirsty.**

PRAYER (from the Coptic Orthodox liturgy)

> Pray for the raising of the river waters this year,
> that Christ, our Lord,
> may bless it and raise it to its measure,
> grant a cheerful touch
> unto the lands, support the human beings,
> save the cattle
> and forgive us our sins.
> **Kyrie eleison—Lord, have mercy.** (*WE* 31)

Pray for the trees, vegetations,
and land plantations this year,
that Christ, our Lord, may bless them
to grow and bring forth
plentiful fruit, have compassion upon his creation
and forgive us our sins.
Kyrie Eleison—Lord, have mercy.
Accord, O Lord, a cheerful touch upon the earth,
water it,
and dispose our life as deemed fit.
Crown this year with your goodness,
for the sake of the poor of your people,
the widow, the orphan, the stranger,
and for our sake.
For our eyes are focused upon you, our hope,
and seek your holy name.
You provide us our food in due course.
Deal with us, O Lord, according to your goodness,
you, the feeder of everybody.
Fill our hearts with joy and grace,
that, as we always have sufficiently of all things,
we grow in every good deed. Amen.
Kyrie eleison—Lord, have mercy.

A prayer from Somalia:

O God, give us rain,
we are in misery, we suffer with our children.
Send us the clouds that bring us rain.
We pray you, O Lord, our father,
to send us the rain. Amen.

May the road rise to meet you,
May the wind be always at your back.
May the sun shine warm upon your face.
May the rains fall softly upon your fields until we meet again.
May God hold you in the hollow of his hand.

(*Old Gaelic blessing*)

HYMN 301

Like a mighty river flowing

Drugs

During the 1960s, middle-class kids and university students brought youth culture, drugs, and music into a trinity. Not every person by any means smoked dope, took LSD, or sought for cheaper 'highs'. Drug-taking was a radical act of rebellion. By the mid-1980s, drug culture became far more general. It began the process which has meant that in the 1990s drugs are a feature of most young people's awareness. At its most obvious, much of the 1990s music scene, based in the phenomenal growth of clubs, is about disorientation. The best-known drug is Ecstasy, if only because the press has reported several stories of young people dying, in part due to this drug. The pop fraternity prefer cocaine, and some heroin, and so it might be said of the young professional class.

Some countries, especially the United States, spend a phenomenal sum in fighting drug barons and cartels. In the early 1990s H M Customs in the UK spent £150 million a year in an effort to prevent the importing of drugs, but drug-selling is about big money. Diamorphine BP (pure heroin) in the same year cost £5.86 per gram through the British National Health Service. A street dealer was selling for over £200. Many people, though, are questioning the efficacy of the war on drugs, for they say it does no more than increase the profits of illicit sellers. Meantime many people are worried that even within the youth community there is little concern about drug abuse.

READINGS

James 1.12–16

Blessed is anyone who endures temptation. Such a one has stood the test and will receive the crown of life that the Lord has promised to those who love him. No one, when tempted, should say, 'I am being tempted by God'; for God cannot be tempted by evil and he himself tempts no one. But one is tempted by one's own desire, being lured and enticed by it; then, when that desire has conceived, it gives birth to sin, and that sin, when it is fully grown, gives birth to death. Do not be deceived, my beloved.

Romans 12.1–2

I appeal to you therefore, my brothers and sisters, by the mercies of God, to present your bodies as a living sacrifice, holy and acceptable to God, which is your spiritual worship. Do not be conformed to this world, but be transformed by the renewing of your minds, so that you may discern what is the will of God—what is good and acceptable and perfect.

HYMN 137

Before the world began

PRAYER

**Father, I dance, I relish the movement and freedom of my body.
I love sound. I hear with joy so many musics.
I swing. I feel the beat and pulse of music. I hear the mood of the moment. I share and blend with others and find an exciting harmony. I thank you for creating such times and moments of wonder and even sheer exhaustion.**

> **Give me moments and times to think and reflect,
> Give me the strength of identity and respect for my head, mind, and body,
> Give me the strength to face with firmness, voices and forces that would devalue me for money,
> Fill my conscience, occupy my mind with your will, your purpose,
> Your design for me and others.
> Amen.**

HYMN 73

Lord of the dance

Fashion

According to *Arena* magazine, a British gentlemen's quarterly, Italian fashion is the best in the world. Obviously such a view would be disputed by the French, Japanese, American, and British who all boast vibrant balance of payments from their fashion industries. But while fashion may talk about the 'classic' whether in style or garment, fashion is never static, with boundaries between good and bad taste constantly shifting. The world's major yearly fashion shows in New York, Paris, Milan, and London continually tell this story year after year. But fashion is not necessarily tied to money and designer name and label. The dance and club scene, the sudden outbursts of particular music styles such as beat, rock 'n' roll, punk, and grunge can produce idiosyncratic styles at rock bottom prices. In terms of names and contrast, the fashion industry's bible, *W Magazine*, suggests Jackie Onassis and Madonna as the polar-opposite style icons. Apart from mere fashion statement and retail considerations, fashion has other more settled areas. There is a plethora of materials and fabrics, some of which are man-made, an endless panoply of colour and dyes, of prints, cuts, and styles. Patricia Lester, a top-of-the-range designer, says of her work, 'Scarves, clothes, interiors; they are all just vehicles for fabric. The advantage of clothes is that they will come alive and move. With interiors, fabrics echo each other and work together'—such is the story of a fashion disciple.

HYMN 172

Praise God, from whom all blessings flow

READING

Ezekiel 16.7b–14

You grew up and became tall and arrived at full womanhood; your breasts were formed, and your hair had grown; yet you were naked and bare.

I passed by you again and looked on you; you were at the age for love. I spread the edge of my cloak over you, and covered your nakedness: I pledged myself to you and entered into a covenant with you, says the Lord God, and you became mine. Then I bathed you with water and washed off the blood from you, and anointed you with oil. I clothed you with embroidered cloth and with sandals of fine leather; I bound you in fine linen and covered you with rich fabric. I adorned you with ornaments: I put bracelets on your arms, a chain on your neck, a ring on your nose, ear-rings in your ears, and a beautiful crown upon your head. You were adorned with gold and silver, while your clothing was of fine linen, rich fabric, and embroidered cloth. You had choice flour and honey and oil for food. You grew exceedingly beautiful, fit to be a queen. Your fame spread among the nations on account of your beauty, for it was perfect because of my splendour that I had bestowed upon you, says the Lord God.

PRAYER

O give thanks to the Lord, for he is good.
We give thanks for the myriad colours of the world,
O give thanks to the Lord, for he is good.
We give thanks for clothes: textures and fabrics,
We give thanks for endless styles and cuts,
We give thanks for a multitude of shapes and designs,
We give thanks for the art of tailoring,
for detail, precision, and love of quality.
We give thanks for the rituals of dressing,
and the joy that it can bring.
O give thanks to the Lord, for he is good.
Save us, good Lord from the tyranny of fashion
that favours only the presumed ideal;
Save us from blindly following trends,
give us confidence to create our own style;
Save us from fashion fixation, where getting dressed is a political statement,
Let our clothes express an awareness of ourselves.

To the God who creates, and hates sham, the short-changed, and the deliberate second-rate, be all praise and glory. Amen.

HYMN 140

God is love

Football Culture

The year 1996 saw football's first theme restaurant. Often football is the subject of a less sanguine story. One moment the sports pages, and sometimes even the news columns, speak of violence at football grounds, and anti-social behaviour by a few supposed fans, and the next they write of footballing geniuses.

There are those who speak of football being more important than life or death—the extraordinarily successful Bill Shankly, once manager of the equally triumphant English team, Liverpool F.C., is one who has talked in this manner. Within the professional game there are those who approach their life and game from a religious, and often specifically Christian perspective. Dave Merrington, one-time manager of Southampton, tells of how it was that the death of his grandmother from cancer gave him a different perspective and dimension. He observed and marvelled at the way in which her faith sustained her through the most difficult times, and it helped him find his.

Many a teenager idolizing the amazing football skills and now managerial knowledge of the England football team supremo, Glenn Hoddle, must be totally unaware that such a gifted sportsman might feel he had few answers to the central problems of life and living. After all, would they not say that football skill and success constitute the very essence of a happy existence? Yet Hoddle sought religious faith, and having found it, he speaks of its personal influence. Hoddle is aware of the tensions involved in the modern game, with its high financial rewards and commercial demands, and the almost unbearable cravings of fans for success. Christian faith offers him, and Merrington, character, strength, and an inner peace that enables them to rise above the sometimes irksome and negative attitudes that are thrown their way by disgruntled fans.

PRAYER

Remind us, good Lord, that all gifts and benefits come from you.
Make us thankful and humble.

Remind us, good Lord, that all gifts and benefits are for sharing.
Make us ready to give and support those of less ability.

Remind us, good Lord, that winning should come from honesty.
Make us aware that an aggressive and positive frame of mind should be balanced.

Remind us, good Lord, that competition is not about finding enemies.

Make us considerate and respectful of others that in victory or defeat the love for what we do can unite over and above all else.

HYMN 254

There's a quiet understanding

READINGS

Colossians 3.11–14

In that renewal there is no longer Greek and Jew, circumcised and uncircumcised, barbarian, Scythian, slave and free; but Christ is all and in all!

As God's chosen ones, holy and beloved, clothe yourselves with compassion, kindness, humility, meekness, and patience. Bear with one another and, if anyone has a complaint against another, forgive each other; just as the Lord has forgiven you, so you also must forgive. Above all, clothe yourselves with love, which binds everything together in perfect harmony.

Colossians 4.5

Conduct yourselves wisely towards outsiders, making the most of the time. Let your speech always be gracious, seasoned with salt, so that you may know how you ought to answer everyone.

HYMN 208

I will enter his gates

Hiroshima Day

(6 August—also Feast of the Transfiguration)

Two clouds are in our minds today. One is that huge mushroom cloud which erupted over the city of Hiroshima on 6 August 1945, ushering in the new age of atomic terror. The other is the cloud that came down to overshadow the glory of Christ on the Mount of Transfiguration. It seems more than an ironic coincidence that the day for commemorating these two events should fall on the same date. The cloud of human sin hides the glory of God. Yet through the cloud we still hear the voice of God pointing to the one human being who has revealed God's glory to us. 'This is my beloved Son, in whom I take delight,' the voice says, 'Listen to him.'

> Had we but hearkened to Thy word,
> And followed in Thy way,
> The clouds would ne'er have gathered now,
> Nor darkness shroud the way.

MUSIC

Solemn Melody: H. Walford Davies

In Hiroshima this day is commemorated every year in a ceremony where a gong calls all the people to prayer. In their prayers they express their grief for the hundreds of thousands who were killed or permanently maimed as a result of the dropping of the atomic bomb. They ask for forgiveness for all the evil that caused such suffering. And they reaffirm their resolve to work for peace. As a symbol of that resolve, a flock of doves is released, and as they go soaring up into the heavens they seem to carry the prayers and the hopes of the people with them. Let us lift our hearts towards that vision of peace in our hymn.

HYMN 364

Let there be love shared among us

READING

Matthew 17.1–8

Jesus took with him Peter and James and his brother John and led them up a high mountain, by themselves. And he was transfigured before them, and his face shone like the sun, and his clothes became dazzling white. Suddenly there appeared to them Moses and Elijah, talking with him. Then Peter said to Jesus, 'Lord, it is good for us to be here; if you wish, I will make three dwellings here, one for you, one for Moses, and one for Elijah.' While he was still speaking, suddenly a bright cloud overshadowed them, and from the cloud a voice said, 'This is my Son, the Beloved; with him I am well pleased; listen to him!' When the disciples heard this, they fell to the ground and were overcome by fear. But Jesus came and touched them, saying, 'Get up and do not be afraid.' And when they looked up, they saw no one except Jesus himself alone.

Silence

A gong sounds

PRAYERS

Lord Jesus Christ, we confess that we are afraid, we are afraid of the darkness of the cloud that hides from the world the glory of your love. Help us to see beyond the cloud the radiance of your presence and to worship you in all your majesty. Help us then to come down with you from the mountain top into our overshadowed world. Teach us how to live here in obedience to your word and in the peace that you have promised to bestow.

A prayer for forgiveness used regularly in Coventry cathedral:

> The hatred which divides nation from nation, race from race, class from class,
> Response: **Father, forgive.**
> The covetous desires of people and nations to possess what is not their own.
> **Father, forgive.**
> The greed which exploits the labours of others and lays waste the earth,
> **Father, forgive.**
> Our envy of the welfare and happiness of others,

Father, forgive.

Our indifference to the plight of the homeless and the refugee,

Father, forgive.

The lust which uses for ignoble ends the bodies of men and
women,

Father, forgive.

The pride which leads us to trust in ourselves and not in God,

Father, forgive.

Chant: Look, the Lamb of God (*WE* 106)

And as we are together, praying for peace, let us be truly with each
other . . .

Chant

Let us be aware of the source of being common to us all and to all
living things.

Chant

Let us pray that all living beings may realize that they are brothers
and sisters, nourished from the same source of life.

Chant

Let us pray that we ourselves cease to be the cause of suffering to
each other.

Chant

Let us resolve to live in a way which will not deprive other living
beings of air, water, food, shelter, or the chance to live.

Chant

With humility, and with awareness of the sufferings that are still
going on around us, let us pray for the establishment of peace in
our hearts and on earth. Amen.

> (Based on a prayer by the Venerable Thich Nhat Hanh, in
> *Prayers for Peace*, 29)

HYMN 337

Make me a channel of your peace

May the peace of God which passes all understanding, keep your
hearts and minds in the knowledge and love of God, and of Jesus
Christ our Lord: And the blessing of God Almighty, the Father,
the Son and the Holy Spirit, be amongst us and remain with us
always. Amen.

Hostages

People say that no news is better than bad news. It does not feel like that when a person is seized and taken away in captivity and cut off from all contact with family and friends. Those who have experienced that kind of isolation, however, tell of how the awareness that they had not been forgotten, and that people were still caring about them, could penetrate the walls of their prison and keep hope alive. So even when we have no news and no means of contact, we keep up the vigil of prayer, believing that in some way our prayers can surround and support those who are alone, and can be one means towards bringing about their release.

We begin our worship today therefore by lighting candles as a focus of our prayers:

(*Lighting candles*) I light a candle for [name]
I light a candle for [name]
I light a candle for all in captivity, whom we do not know but whose names are known to God.

God is light, and in him is no darkness at all. The light shines in the darkness and the darkness cannot overcome it.

HYMN 143

Christ, whose glory fills the skies

PRAYER

O God, source of all light, let the rays of your presence illuminate even the darkest dungeons of our world. Keep the flame of hope burning in those who are held captive and in those who are working for their release, and grant that soon the day of deliverance shall dawn, and the captives emerge into the light of liberty. Amen.

READING

St Paul and his companion, Silas, experienced imprisonment themselves. But though their limbs were bound in fetters, their spirits knew the freedom of faith, and the infection of their good courage spread even to their jailers.

Acts 16.25–34

About midnight Paul and Silas were praying and singing hymns to God, and the prisoners were listening to them. Suddenly there was an earthquake, so violent that the foundations of the prison were shaken; immediately all the doors were opened and everyone's chains were unfastened. When the jailer woke up and saw the prison doors wide open, he drew his sword and was about to kill himself, since he supposed that the prisoners had escaped. But Paul shouted in a loud voice, 'Do not harm yourself, for we are all here.' The jailer called for lights, and rushing in, he fell down trembling before Paul and Silas. Then he brought them outside and said, 'Sirs, what must I do to be saved?' They answered, 'Believe on the Lord Jesus, and you will be saved, you and your household.' They spoke the word of the Lord to him and to all who were in his house. At the same hour of the night he took them and washed their wounds; then he and his whole family were baptized without delay. He brought them up into the house and set food before them; and he and his entire household rejoiced that he had become a believer in God.
Thanks be to God.

RESPONSE

Hallelujah, Hallelujah (Zimbabwe) (*WE* 61)

INTERCESSIONS

Let us pray for those who hold others captive, trying to see them as God sees them, vulnerable human beings, with their fears and their fanaticism, but also capable of kindness:

Compassionate God, we pray for those whose hearts are so fettered by hatred that they fail to be moved by compassion for their fellow human beings. Set them free from their fears so that they might set others free from their bonds, and grant to them even this day a generosity of spirit that shall express itself in some act of kindness towards those whom they hold captive. Lord, hear our prayer.
Response: **O Lord hear my prayer, come and listen to me** (Taizé)

Let us pray for those who are anxious for their loved ones:
Loving God, we pray for the families and friends of those who are
missing. Give them good courage, a strong faith, and patience to
persevere in prayer, and in protest, until the day that the prison
door opens and their loved ones return home. Lord, hear our
prayer.
Response: **O Lord hear my prayer, come and listen to me**
Let us pray for all who are working to bring about the release of
hostages: God of all power, we pray for those who have
responsibility and influence. Give them wisdom in negotiation,
persistence in persuasion, and determination not to give up until
the captives are released and restored to full well-being. Lord, hear
our prayer.
Response: **O Lord hear my prayer, come and listen to me**

The prayer of a prisoner

If the Lord is in prison with me, what do I fear?
Lonely and solitary though I am,
I believe, I praise, I give thanks.

If the Lord is in prison with me, why do I grieve?
The Lord knows my trouble and pain,
to him I entrust my heart and my all,
I believe, I rejoice, I sing.

Hsu T'ien Hsien (*With All God's People*, 47)

God of light, kindle within our hearts a spark of faith, a flame of
hope, a fire of love, that we may be faithful in prayer and thankful
for our freedom. Amen.

Terry Waite, who was for over four years a hostage in Beirut,
spoke of the encouragement that came to him from the one
postcard that reached him, showing a picture of John Bunyan in his
prison cell. Our last hymn expresses the courage which Bunyan and
so many other prisoners have shown in their captivity.

HYMN 350
Who would true valour see

Hunger

'You may find some of these pictures distressing,' said the TV presenter, introducing a film sequence from a famine-stricken area of the world. They were compelling pictures—compelling a compassion which in some people inspired a new commitment to aid and emergency relief. But others complained of 'compassion fatigue', a sense of helplessness in the face of a hunger which is not only the result of emergency but is endemic in large areas of the world. We are not helpless. We all have some means of helping to feed the hungry, by the aid we give, by the justice we pursue, by the policies we support and by the way we ourselves live. As one of our modern prophets has put it, 'We all have to learn to live simply in order that others may simply live.'

HYMN 385

When I needed a neighbour, were you there?

READING

To those who have known hunger or thirst, even the plainest food and the clearest water are perceived as great riches, signs of the abundance of God's blessing. The prophets of Israel called people to come closer to God by turning from lives of luxury and greed to a simpler style of living, which would honour God's goodness and enable others to enjoy God's blessing too.

Isaiah 55

Ho, everyone who thirsts, come to the waters;
and you that have no money, come, buy and eat!
Come, buy wine and milk without money and without price.
Why do you spend your money for that which is not bread,
and your labour for that which does not satisfy?
Listen carefully to me, and eat what is good,
and delight yourself in rich food.
Incline your ear, and come to me;
listen, so that you may live.

I will make with you an everlasting covenant,
my steadfast, sure love for David.
See, I made him a witness to the peoples,
a leader and commander for the peoples.
See, you shall call nations that you do not know,
and nations that do not know you shall run to you,
because of the Lord your God, the Holy One of Israel,
for he has glorified you.

RESPONSE

Glory to God (Peruvian acclamation)   (*WE* 31)

'The only way God dare appear to a hungry person is in the form
of bread,' said Mahatma Gandhi. A poem from India echoes his
words:

> Every noon at twelve
> in the blazing heat
> God comes to me
> In the form of
> two hundred grams of gruel.
> I know him in every grain,
> I taste him in every lick.
> I commune with him as I gulp
> For he keeps me alive, with
> Two hundred grams of gruel.
>
> (Quoted in *Struggle to be the Sun again*
> p. 72 by Chung Hyun Kyung, SCM Press)

INTERCESSIONS

Lord, we pray for those who are the victims of famine. Help us
through their suffering to realize anew our dependence upon one
another, and our need to share from our abundance with their
poverty.
Whatever we do for the least of these, we do for you.
Lord, we pray for those who are risking their lives to transport
food to the hungry and medicines to the sick, and for all aid
workers, who stay at their posts in hospitals and refugee camps in
some of the most dangerous places in our world and refuse to give

way to the threat of violence or the fear of death. Guide and protect them by your presence.

Whatever we do for the least of these, we do for you.

Lord, we pray for all who are striving to promote greater justice in the allocation of the world's resources, for those who seek fairer trade agreements, for those who make decisions about overseas aid, and for those who invest their own wealth in the world's poor.

Whatever we do for the least of these, we do for you.

Grant, O Lord, that I who have never known an empty stomach may ever remember those who have never known a full one; that I who have never known poverty may not forget those who have never known anything else; that I who have never known cold may be aware of those who have never felt warmth; and above all that I, to whom so much has been given, may ever remember those who have so little; and remembering them may I seek to minister to their needs in every way I can, for your dear love's sake. Amen.

(Nadir Dinshaw)

Lord, forgive us if we ever complain of compassion fatigue. When our hearts sink at the sight of so much human suffering, show us something practical we can do in helping to relieve it and give us the will to do it, for your name's sake. Amen.

A Grace Before Food

God, make us more thankful for what we have received, more content with what we have, more mindful of people in need, and more ready to help them in whatever way we can. Amen.

HYMN 190

Jesus the Lord said, I am the bread

Hurricane in the Caribbean

Hurricanes are no strangers in the islands of the Caribbean. They come so frequently that they are given familiar names, called after the letters of the alphabet to indicate the order in which they arrive. But their visit is by no means welcome. They can destroy not only people's homes but their whole livelihood, sweeping away the banana plants or sugar cane on which so much of the Caribbean economy depends.

'God is no stranger' either, to the Caribbean. That's the title of a book of prayers gathered from the spontaneous outpourings of the heart from Christians in Haiti. They have come to know Christ as One who shares their daily lives and understands their deepest needs. So they find it natural to pray what are sometimes called arrow prayers, short sentences directed to God in simple language, expressing the need of the moment.

ARROW PRAYERS (read with brief pauses in between)

Lord, how glad we are that we don't hold you, but that you hold us.

Lord, if we are alive today, in spite of hurricanes, hunger, and sickness, we should say, 'Thank you, Lord, we must be here for a purpose.'

Father, they say we are the poorest country in the world. Thank you Father. May we also be poor in spirit that we may inherit the Kingdom of God.

Lord, there's a big devil called discouragement. We ask you to send him away because he's bothering us.

No one keeps on trying something if he never makes progress. If Satan keeps tempting us, it's because we keep giving him some encouragement.

Lord, suffering is the Potter's wheel which turns us in the Potter's hand of love and affection.

Lord, help us to sow good seed since we will be the ones eating from the harvest.

Father, a cold wind seems to have chilled us. Wrap us in the
blanket of your word and warm us up a bit. Amen.

(From *God is no Stranger*, published by Haiti Baptist Mission)

HYMN 259
What a friend we have in Jesus

READING
As we think of the Caribbean islands with their majestic but cruel
mountains and the even greater mountain of human suffering,
caused through the hurricane, we turn to Psalm 121.

PSALM
I lift up my eyes to the hills—from where will my help come?
My help comes from the Lord, who made heaven and earth.
He will not let your foot be moved;
he who keeps you will not slumber.
He who keeps Israel will neither slumber nor sleep.
The Lord is your keeper;
the Lord is your shade at your right hand.
The sun shall not strike you by day, nor the moon by night.
The Lord will keep you from all evil; he will keep your life.
The Lord will keep your going out and your coming in
from this time on and for evermore.

PRAYERS
Response: **Kumba yah, Lord, kumba yah** (possibly meaning 'Come
by here, Lord)
Someone's crying, Lord, crying tears of anguish and loss.
There are tears of bereavement, and tears of bewilderment,
Tears of anxiety and tears of disappointment.
Someone's crying, Lord,
Kumba yah
Someone's dying, Lord, dying of injury, in the ruins of their
home,
Dying of hunger because their crops have been destroyed,
Dying of despair and dying of pain.
Someone's dying, Lord,
Kumba yah

Someone's praying, Lord, praying for help in this time of need,
Praying for support in the months to come,
Praying for the chance to rebuild their lives.
Someone's praying, Lord,
Kumba yah
Lord, hear our prayers and use our lives as a means of answering
them. Amen.

In an affirmation that comes to us from the Caribbean we pray:
We believe in you O God, for you have made the suffering of
humanity your suffering. You have come to establish a kingdom of
the poor and humble. Today we sing to you because you are alive,
you have saved us, you have made us free. Alleluia. Amen.

HYMN 175
Lord, thy Church on earth is seeking

And may the God of hope fill the people of the Caribbean with all
joy and peace in believing, that they may abound in hope through
the power of the Holy Spirit. Amen.

Law and Order

In London alone, during 1995, 1.6 million emergency calls were made. Most calls are answered quickly and efficiently, and many of them are not emergencies in any true sense of the word. The Metropolitan Police claim considerable success in meeting crime with various schemes, almost invariably given a name, such as Operation Bumblebee, spearheading their campaign. They talk of the incidence of burglary in the British capital dropping, and the amount of stolen property recovered rising. They speak of a higher arrest rate and a greater number of offences detected. Their overall aim rests in making major inroads against crime and making the capital a better and safer place.

Certainly 'law and order' is the contentious issue upon which all British political parties profess strong interest. Their antennae are tuned to the seeming disquiet amongst people of all ages that safety of citizens to walk about their local and wider areas is under threat from muggers and rapists. Statistical evidence suggests that the real, as against supposed threat is minimal, but the popular view flies against the cold analysis of figures. Maintaining law and order is not only a problem for major cities and their inner areas, whether in Britain or world-wide, for many speak of a breakdown in civilized behaviour in rural and urban areas. In terms of his own society and culture, Jesus had respect for Old Testament teaching with its strong emphasis upon righteousness, and equal distaste for wrong-doing. Yet he opposed excessive legalism that placed a stranglehold upon people's lives. Paul saw the 'law' acting as a 'schoolmaster' to lead people to an understanding of Jesus. Paul talked of the Christian guided by love. Both Matthew and James saw Christianity as a new law with the purpose of producing a richer life for citizens.

READING

Galatians 3.23–6

Now before faith came, we were imprisoned and guarded under the law until faith would be revealed. Therefore the law was our disciplinarian until Christ came, so that we might be justified by faith. But now that faith has come, we are no longer subject to a disciplinarian, for in Christ Jesus you are all children of God through faith.

HYMN 284

Abba Father

PRAYERS

May our lives be but mirrors of your justice.
May we see your image in each one.

We acknowledge our own culpability.
We see destruction, hurt, and sin.
We are part of a society often torn apart.
We are caught up in the structures of injustice.
We seek forgiveness.

We pray for the victims of violence;
those whose lives have been shattered by the experience.
We pray for those whose homes have been ransacked
and who in consequence feel deeply uneasy.
We pray for those who walk the streets in fear
and who live under great stress.

We pray for those who work for law agencies;
Give them authority tempered by compassion.
We pray for police officers often placed in uncongenial situations;
Give them courage and assertiveness tempered by care.

You are the giver of life and law.
You have taught us that if we do not love our brother and sister
then we cannot love you.
Teach us to know and love your ways.

HYMN 314

Seek ye first the kingdom of God

Life Story

E very week on the BBC we can eavesdrop a little on the lives of people.

On the radio, there is the long-lasting *Desert Island Discs*. At first sight it seems no more than a pleasant conversation game. Someone well-known is told they are marooned on a desert island. To pass the time of day they have with them eight of their favourite recordings. But on second sight, it is not just a simple playing of some records with bits of conversation thrown in to break up the music input. What we get is a little filling-in of the remark 'Tell me what you sing, and I'll tell you who you are.' What we hear is a mini-autobiography, often with the artist choosing music from his or her many decades of life. Memories, events, conversations, and feelings are recalled and if some are universal then we, the listener, might well find recollections from our experience coming into our consciousness.

Another programme with 'a story to tell' is BBC Television's *Songs Of Praise* which, in common with *Desert Island Discs*, has had a long airtime life. Here, a number of people are interviewed about their lives, or more often than not, a particular life-changing moment. A suitable accompanying hymn is chosen. Again, both the recollection and choice of hymn might stir within us our own past and what an event meant.

It is generally agreed among all the personal sciences and many religions, that each of us needs to tell our story. In this act of worship, invite two or three people to give their own testimony as to how they found faith.

HYMN 288

Blessed assurance

PRAYER

For our lives—
We thank you
For our memories—
We thank you
For times of meaning—
We thank you

For moments of sheer joy—
We thank you.

When there is lack of joy, unrest, a feeling of incompleteness, help us to move beyond so that our faith is in the future. How could a dead person want a living God?

READING

I John 1.1–4

We declare to you what was from the beginning, what we have heard, what we have seen with our eyes, what we have looked at and touched with our hands, concerning the word of life—this life was revealed, and we have seen it and testify to it, and declare to you the eternal life that was with the Father and was revealed to us—we declare to you what we have seen and heard so that you also may have fellowship with us; and truly our fellowship is with the Father and with his Son Jesus Christ. We are writing these things so that our joy may be complete.

HYMN 241

O for a thousand tongues to sing

Marriage

The Prophet, by Kahlil Gibran, is full of wise words. In writing about marriage he says, 'Let there be spaces in your togetherness . . . Stand together, yet not too near together: for the pillars of the temple stand apart, and the oak tree and the cypress grow not in each other's shadow.' In describing married love, he writes elsewhere that to love means:

'To wake at dawn with a winged heart and give thanks for
    another day of loving;
To rest at the noon hour and meditate on love's ecstasy;
To return home at eventide with gratitude;
And then to sleep with a prayer for the beloved in your heart
    and a song of praise upon your lips.'

That same sentiment is expressed in our first hymn

HYMN 303

Lord of all hopefulness, Lord of all joy

READING

St John records that the first of the signs of the glory of Jesus was given at a wedding feast.

John 2.1–10

On the third day there was a wedding in Cana of Galilee, and the mother of Jesus was there. Jesus and his disciples had also been invited to the wedding. When the wine gave out, the mother of Jesus said to him, 'They have no wine.' And Jesus said to her, 'Woman, what concern is that to you and to me? My hour has not yet come.' His mother said to the servants, 'Do whatever he tells you.' Now standing there were six stone water-jars for the Jewish rites of purification, each holding twenty or thirty gallons. Jesus said to them, 'Fill the jars with water.' And they filled them up to the brim. He said to them, 'Now draw some out, and take it to the chief steward.' So they took it. When the steward tasted the water that had become wine, and did not know where it came from (though the servants who had drawn the water knew), the steward called the bridegroom and said to him, 'Everyone serves the good wine first, and then the inferior wine after the guests have become drunk. But you have kept the good wine until now.'

PRAYERS

Not for me is the love that knows no restraint, but like the foaming
    wine, having burst its vessel in a moment, would run to waste.
Send me the love which is cool and pure, like your rain that blesses
    the thirsty earth and fills the homely earthen jars.
Send me the love that would soak down into the centre of being, and
    from there would spread like the unseen sap through the
    branching tree of life, giving birth to its fruits and flowers.
Send me the love that keeps the heart still with the fullness of peace.

                    (Rabindranath Tagore, *OBP* 895)

Lord, you were present with us at our marriage; stay with us throughout our lives together. When the first heady wine of our love for one another runs out, replenish us with fresh supplies of your love which becomes richer, maturer, sweeter as the years go by. So may we go on to discover greater delight in our marriage and a closer companionship together with you to the very end of our days. Amen.

We pray for those whose marriages are at risk or are breaking down. Encourage them to seek help from wise counsel, and to recognize the hurt they are doing to one another and to all who love them. Grant them the grace of a new beginning, whether it be together or apart, and may there be no bitterness nor recrimination, but only the desire to do what is best for one another and for all who love them. Amen.

Lord Jesus, who brought such joy to the wedding at Cana, we ask your blessing on those who are engaged to be married, that there may be truth at the beginning of their lives together, unselfishness all the way, and perseverance to the end. May their hopes be realized and their love for each other deepen and grow, that through them your name may be glorified. Amen.

                    (Mothers' Union)

Lord, we pray for all those to whom our lives are bound by any special tie, either by nature or by choice, that we may love one another as you love us. Make us slow to anger and swift to forgive. Help us to be honest with one another and to honour each other's integrity. Give us joy in our relationship throughout our lives, and when we are finally parted by death may we look forward to being together with you in the glorious kingdom of your eternal love. Amen.

HYMN 299
Lead us, heavenly Father, lead us

Mental Illness

Too often people who are mentally ill are shunned by others who are afraid of them, or isolated from the community for their own protection. Throughout the centuries, mentally disturbed people have been feared, mocked, even regarded as being possessed by evil spirits. Such was the attitude in the days when Jesus was on earth. He recognized their isolation, spoke to them without fear, and was able to calm their troubled spirits. We pray for that same healing influence now, on all who suffer from sickness of the mind and for those who have become the victims of mentally disturbed people.

HYMN 139

Go, tell it on the mountain

PRAYER

We bring into your presence, Lord, whose who suffer from mental illness, dementia, or depression. May they all find calming comfort through the hands of people caring for them. Help them to be aware that you, who brought order out of chaos, can eventually restore peace of mind even to the most disordered spirits. We ask this through the name of the one who 'makes the wounded spirit whole', Jesus Christ our Lord.

READING

Luke 8.26–39

Jesus deals with a man who was a danger both to himself and to others:

Then they arrived at the country of the Gerasenes, which is opposite Galilee. As he stepped out on land, a man of the city who had demons met him. For a long time he had worn no clothes, and he did not live in a house but in the tombs. When he saw Jesus, he fell down before him and shouted at the top of his voice, 'What have you to do with me, Jesus, Son of the Most High God? I beg you, do not torment me'—for Jesus had commanded the unclean spirit to come out of the man. (For many times it had seized him; he was kept under guard and bound with chains and shackles, but he would break the bonds and be driven by the demon into the wilds.)

Jesus then asked him, 'What is your name?' He said 'Legion'; for many demons had entered him. They begged him not to order them to go back into the abyss.

Now there on the hillside a large herd of swine was feeding; and the demons begged Jesus to let them enter these. So he gave them permission. Then the demons came out of the man and entered the swine, and the herd rushed down the steep bank into the lake and was drowned.

When the swineherds saw what had happened, they ran off and told it in the city and in the country. Then people came out to see what had happened, and when they came to Jesus, they found the man from whom the demons had gone out sitting at the feet of Jesus, clothed and in his right mind. And they were afraid. Those who had seen it told them how the one who had been possessed by demons had been healed. Then all the people of the surrounding country of the Gerasenes asked Jesus to leave them; for they were seized with great fear. So he got into the boat and returned. The man from whom the demons had gone begged that he might be with him; but Jesus sent him away, saying, 'Return to your home, and declare how much God has done for you.' So he went away, proclaiming throughout the city how much Jesus had done for him.

CHANT

Nada te turbe—Nothing can trouble you (*WE* 139)

PRAYERS

Lord Jesus, who looked with compassion on the man whom others feared, and saw through his inner torment to the right mind within, we pray for those whose minds are so disturbed that they are unable to pray for themselves. Cast out from their hearts the demons of rage and violence, and grant that, amid the many voices that torment them, they may hear your voice, saying, 'Peace, be still'.

Nada te turbe

Lord Jesus, who shed tears with those who wept, we weep for loved ones whose minds have become so clouded by dementia that they seem to have become strangers even to those closest to them. Help us to continue to respect the personalities hidden behind the mask of illness, to go on loving them and showing them the care they once showed to others. Give us the faith to see, beyond the deterioration of their physical and mental powers, their spiritual needs being met by the compassionate presence of God mediated through human patience and through our prayers.

Nada te turbe

Lord Jesus, the healer, we pray for all who care for the mentally disturbed. Give wisdom to psychiatrists who seek to probe the mysteries of the human mind; give patient skill to the nurses who work in hospitals for the mentally ill; give greater understanding to the communities into whose care so many disturbed people are now entrusted; and grant particular grace to families affected by mental illness, that love may learn to drive out fear and hope help to banish despair.

Nada te turbe

Lord, keep us ever mindful of that perfect love which casts out all our fears and grant to us that stability which comes from trusting in your steadfastness. Help us to lose our fear of mental illness and by our love for those who suffer from it may we enable them to find healing and peace of mind, through Jesus Christ our Lord. Amen.

HYMN 146

How sweet the name of Jesus sounds

CLOSING PRAYER

Lord, when it is dark and we cannot feel your presence, and nothing seems real any more, and we are tempted to give up trying, help us to remember that you are never really absent, and to trust you still, so that we may rest in your love, and know that underneath are the everlasting arms of your mercy, now and always. Amen.

(NEM p. 105)

A Cry for Mercy

O ne simple word is the theme of our worship today. It is a beautiful word, one heard on the lips of sinners and saints, of criminals and suppliants—mercy. It is derived from the Latin word 'merces', which means 'reward'. In French it means 'thank you', the gratitude one feels for undeserved reward. 'Mercy', says Portia, the judge in *The Merchant of Venice*, is an attribute of God.

> And earthly power doth then show likest God's
> When mercy seasons justice

Today, as we have in mind people who stand under judgment in the courts, we reflect on our own need both to receive mercy and to show it. We celebrate first the mercy in the heart of God.

HYMN 39

Tell out, my soul, the greatness of the Lord!

To Mercy, Pity, Peace and Love
All pray in their distress,
And to these virtues of delight
Return their thankfulness

For Mercy has a human heart,
Pity a human face,
And Love, the human form divine,
And Peace, the human dress

Then every one, of every clime,
That prays in his distress,
Prays to the human form divine,
Love, Mercy, Pity, Peace.

So, says the poet William Blake, 'wherever mercy, love and pity dwell, there God is dwelling too'. That same simple creed is the theme of the Letter of St James, for whom every human being had divine worth and deserved to be treated with the dignity and mercy which God bestows on us all.

READING

James 2.8–13

You do well if you really fulfil the royal law according to the scripture, 'You shall love your neighbour as yourself.' But if you show partiality, you commit sin and are convicted by the law as transgressors. For whoever keeps the whole law but fails in one point has become accountable for all of it. For the one who said, 'You shall not commit adultery', also said, 'You shall not murder.' Now if you do not commit adultery but if you murder, you have become a transgressor of the law. So speak and so act as those who are to be judged by the law of liberty. For judgment will be without mercy to anyone who has shown no mercy; mercy triumphs over judgment.

PRAYERS

You have shown us O God what is good. Enable us to perform what you require: to do justly, to love mercy, and to walk humbly with you, our Lord and our God.

For our incapacity to feel the sufferings of others, and our ability to live comfortably with injustice and exploitation:
Lord, have mercy upon us; **Christ have mercy upon us.**
For the self-righteousness which prizes status, and the self-interest which strangles compassion:
Lord, have mercy upon us; **Christ have mercy upon us.**
For our failures in community, our lack of understanding, for being too swift to condemn and too slow to forgive:
Lord, have mercy upon us; **Christ have mercy upon us.**

(Prayer from South Africa)

Lord, we thank you that you were known as the friend of publicans and sinners. We pray for those who feel outcast or marginalized, that they may find themselves befriended and accepted in a welcoming and inclusive community.
Lord, in your mercy; **hear our prayer.**
Lord, we thank you that no one is beyond the reach of your mercy and grace. May those who feel themselves disgraced or humiliated be treated with that dignity which is their God-given birthright.
Lord, in your mercy; **hear our prayer.**

Lord, we thank you that you enrich the poor with the gift of faith and the promise of the Kingdom. May their faith be fulfilled as they see the signs of that Kingdom here on earth in our compassion and in our readiness to share all your gifts.
Lord, in your mercy; **hear our prayer.**

And we bring to the throne of mercy those who particularly need our prayers today. We pray for those whose needs are obvious to us—those in our streets who are homeless; those we see on our television screens who are hungry; those whose illness or distress make headline news. We pray for those whom we do not see and too easily forget—the millions in our war-torn world who depend on our mercy and on our commitment to work for justice and for peace.
Lord, hear our prayer, **and let our cry come unto you.**
We pray for all who this day must pronounce judgment on those who have been convicted of crime. May they so administer justice as to preserve order and so show mercy as to provide hope.
Lord, hear our prayer, **and let our cry come unto you.**
And may our prayers for mercy teach us all to render the deeds of mercy, for the sake of the Everlasting Mercy.
So may mercy, pity, peace, and love be with us all this day and evermore. Amen.

HYMN 23
The kingdom of God

Public and Private Morality

In the midst of the present confused discussion of personal morality and social ethics we do well to recall that our codes of conduct have their origins in the Book of Law that dates back to the time of Moses. When the children of Israel were wandering in the wilderness in their newly won freedom from slavery, they were given guidelines as to how they were to live together in a just and ordered society. They believed that Book of Law to be so basic to their personal and communal life that in Jewish tradition they have always treated the law itself as coming from the very mouth of God.

HYMN 181

Lord, thy word abideth

PRAYER

O God, the guide and inspiration of all humanity, we thank you for teaching us the laws of life, and we rejoice that you have given us the power to choose how we shall live. Though you are one, you have spoken in a thousand tongues for all to hear. We give thanks for the sages and teachers of all the ages, who have brought many to a deeper understanding of you and of your law. Help us, O God, so to live that our daily conduct may reveal the sincerity and integrity of our faith, and that we may continue to give witness to your truth among all people. For your name's sake. Amen.

(Union of Liberal and Progressive Synagogues)

READING

Our reading is from one of the five books of the law, the Book of Exodus, chapter 20:

Then God spoke all these words:
I am the Lord your God who brought you out of the land of Egypt, out of the house of slavery; you shall have no other gods before me.
Response: **Lord, help us to keep this law.**

You shall not make for yourself an idol, whether in the form of anything that is in heaven above, or that is on the earth beneath, or that is in the water under the earth. You shall not bow down to them nor worship them.

Lord, help us to keep this law.

You shall not make wrongful use of the name of the Lord your God, for the Lord will not acquit anyone who misuses his name.

Lord, help us to keep this law.

Remember the sabbath day and keep it holy.

Lord, help us to keep this law.

Honour your father and your mother, so that your days may be long in the land that the Lord your God is giving you.

Lord, help us to keep this law.

You shall not murder.

Lord, help us to keep this law.

You shall not commit adultery.

Lord, help us to keep this law.

You shall not steal.

Lord, help us to keep this law.

You shall not bear false witness against your neighbour.

Lord, help us to keep this law.

You shall not covet your neighbour's wife, or male or female slave, or ox, or donkey, or anything that belongs to your neighbour.

Lord, write all these laws in our hearts, we beseech you.

'Who shall ascend the hill of the Lord?' asks the psalmist, 'and who shall stand in his holy place? Those who have clean hands and pure hearts, who do not lift up their souls to what is false, and do not swear deceitfully. They will receive blessing from the Lord, and vindication from the God of their salvation.'

PRAYERS

Lord, we confess that we have sinned against your laws.
For failing to show proper reverence towards you,
and for idolizing the works of our own hands,
Lord, forgive us.
For working too hard, and resting too little;
For failing to honour those who are retired or unemployed,
Lord, forgive us.

For our outbursts of anger,
our secret lusts,
our greed at the expense of others,
Lord, forgive us.
For our love of gossip,
our envy of our neighbours,
Lord, forgive us.
Lord, though our sins may be inexcusable, let them not be
unforgivable. Amen.

God of mercy, help us who have been forgiven to be tender and
compassionate towards those who are overtaken by temptation,
considering how we ourselves have fallen in times past and may yet
fall again; and may we neither presume upon your forgiveness by
living carelessly, nor doubt it and be weighed down by guilt, for
your name's sake. Amen.

(*NEM* p. 85)

Almighty God, direct the hearts and minds of those who bear in
their hands the government of the people. Make them to uphold
honour and justice, to restrain evil and oppression, and to seek the
true prosperity of our nation and the welfare of all humanity. Holy
God, may your Spirit enlighten us, cleanse us, and strengthen us
and enable us this day to live to your glory. Amen.

(*NEM* p. 128)

HYMN 15

O worship the King

Obituary

Every day the quality press world-wide devotes space to the obituary. Here, in succinct and literary form, is the story of someone who has died. More often than not, the writer is anonymous. The amount of space allotted may be decided by several factors. First, there is the estimated importance of the deceased; second, there is the quality and standard of the submitted obituary notice; third, there is the amount of space available on the day. Someone of major importance may claim a longer entry than another who might otherwise have received greater coverage. Obituary style appears to have changed in the last ten years to a less formal approach. We are now told in greater detail the human side of someone rather than simply being given a list of awards, degrees, achievements, and last, but not least, the number of the deceased's offspring.

The Bible suggests a concern for primogeniture, with long genealogical lists, as for instance in Genesis 36 or Exodus 20.14–17, while in the New Testament there is Matthew 1.1–17 and Luke 3.23–38. One of the most impressive sweeping surveys of life lived, and influence gained, is in Hebrews 11. But in modern terms, there is nothing resembling the obituary. Scripture writers are of course less concerned with individuals *per se*, than what they achieved for the community and world in faith. The basic teaching of Jesus dwells little on physical death; death is seen as an entrance to eternal life, something utterly natural, and a fellowship with God that promises a completeness unobtainable here on earth.

HYMN 199

For all the saints

READING

Hebrews 12.1–2; 13.5b–6a

Therefore, since we are surrounded by so great a cloud of witnesses, let us also lay aside every weight and the sin that clings so closely, and let us run with perseverance the race that is set before us, looking to Jesus the pioneer and perfecter of our faith, who for the sake of the joy that was set before him endured the cross, disregarding its shame, and has taken his seat at the right hand of the throne of God.

Be content with what you have; for he has said, 'I will never leave you or forsake you.' So we can say with confidence, 'The Lord is my helper; I will not be afraid.'

PRAYERS

May the brilliance of your light illumine the massive obscurities in which we move.

(Teilhard De Chardin)

You who fear Yahweh, praise him!
Entire race of Jacob, glorify him!
Entire race of Israel, revere him!
All people, praise the God of our memories,
All people, praise the God of our past,
All people, praise the God of our future!

We give thanks for those who are named in today's obituary/
obituaries.
We hear for a moment some of the salient points of their lives . . .
We believe that we shall arise from death with a new, undying body,
for our God is the God of the living.

A moment of silence

Glory to God in heaven
and peace to his people on earth.
Amen.

HYMN 202

Light's abode, celestial Salem

Old Age

A man who recently celebrated his ninetieth birthday commented that birthdays come around so swiftly these days that he has now decided to celebrate the decades rather than the years! The older we get the more swiftly time moves. Calendars cease to make sense any more. The distant past is so close. The shorter time ahead gives us glimpses of an eternity where our lives are linked with those who have already gone beyond the limits of time and space but who still seem to be present with us now. We begin with a hymn that celebrates the abiding love of God throughout all our days.

HYMN 22

Through all the changing scenes of life

PRAYERS

O Lord, the first and the last, the beginning and the end:
You who were with us at our birth, be with us through our life.
You who are with us through our life, be with us at our death;
and because your mercy will not leave us then,
grant that we die not, but rise to the life everlasting. Amen
(From the *Cambridge Bede Book*, quoted in *NEM* 123)

Lord we thank you for the blessing of long life, for good memories of those whose love has enriched our lives in the past, for present experience of those whose care supports us now, and for future hope that looks beyond this life to an even fuller life that awaits us in your presence. May we grow old patiently and hopefully, believing that 'the best is yet to be, the last of life, for which the first was made'.

SENTENCES (to be read by old people in the congregation)

Lord, let me not live to be useless.

Lord, give me life till my work be done, and work while my life shall last.

51Lord, you have given me so much, give one thing more—a thankful heart.

Lord, I have time, plenty of time, all the time that you give me,
The years of my life, the days of my years, the hours of my days,
They are all mine.

I am not asking you, Lord, for more time to do this and then that,
But your grace to do conscientiously, in the time that you give me,
What you want me to do. Amen.

(Adapted from Michel Quoist. *Prayers of Life*)

PSALM (some verses from Psalm 90)

Lord, you have been our dwelling-place in all generations.
Before the mountains were brought forth, or ever you had formed the earth and the world,
from everlasting to everlasting you are God.
You turn us back to dust, and say, 'Turn back, you mortals.'
For a thousand years in your sight are like yesterday when it is past, or like a watch in the night.
For all our days pass away under your wrath;
our years come to an end like a sigh.
The days of our life are seventy years, or perhaps eighty, if we are strong;
even then their span is only toil and trouble;
they are soon gone, and we fly away.
So teach us to count our days
that we may gain a wise heart.

INTERCESSIONS

Lord Jesus, you cared for your mother even when you were suffering the agony of the cross, have compassion on those who in their old age have no son or daughter to care for them. When they are lonely, send them companions; when they are frail, give them support; when they are in need of care, provide a safe home with those who will become a loving family for them, for your sake. Amen.

God, bless all those who care for the aged, in home or hospital. We thank you for all good neighbours and community workers, for nurses and carers, for the wardens of homes, and for those who act as advocates for the elderly, campaigning on their behalf. May their reward be the knowledge that they are helping to lift the burden of the years by giving meaning and joy to the present moment, so that the sighs of the old can be sighs of contentment. Amen.

Lord, when the signs of age begin to mark my body (and still more when they touch my mind); when the painful moment comes in which I suddenly awaken to the fact that I am ill or growing old; and above all at the last moment when I feel I am losing hold of myself and am absolutely passive within the hands of the great unknown forces that have formed me; in all those dark moments,

O God, grant that I may understand that it is you who are painfully parting the fibres of my being in order to penetrate to the very marrow of my substance and bear me away within yourself into your eternity. Amen.

(Teilhard de Chardin, *OBP* 133)

So may God, who has helped us in all the years that are past, give us hope for all the years that are to come and bring us safely to our eternal home. Amen.

HYMN 333

Lord, for the years your love has kept and guided

Peace Talks

In a world full of wars and rumours of wars, the news of peace talks being held fills us with a fragile hope which needs to be strengthened by our prayers. In whatever language it is spoken, the word for 'peace' has become a familiar greeting between friends and a word of truce between enemies. It conveys a sense of well-being and expresses a concern for justice. It is an active word, not a passive state. Peace comes to those who earnestly pursue it. All that wealth of meaning is conveyed in the Hebrew greeting 'Shalom'.

SONG (sung as people offer one another a sign of peace)

Shalom, sawidi, a paz   (Latin America)   (*WE* 166)

READING

Through the prophets of many centuries God spoke to the people about peace. The prophet Jeremiah warned them that peace did not come easily. Only by abjuring the horrors of war, repenting of its evils, and seeking the help of God would the nations ever find the way to peace. They must no longer delay. The time had come to bind up the wounds of war.

Jeremiah 8.11–15, 19a, 20–22; 9.1

They have treated the wound of my people carelessly, saying, 'Peace, peace', when there is no peace. They acted shamefully, they committed abomination; yet they were not at all ashamed, they did not know how to blush. Therefore they shall fall among those who fall; at the time when I punish them, they shall be overthrown, says the Lord. When I wanted to gather them, says the Lord, there are no grapes on the vine, nor figs on the fig tree; even the leaves are withered, and what I gave them has passed away from them. Why do we sit still? Gather together, let us go into the fortified cities and perish there; for the Lord our God has doomed us to perish, and has given us poisoned water to drink, because we have sinned against the Lord. We look for peace, but find no good, for a time of healing, but there is terror instead . . .

Hark, the cry of my poor people from far and wide in the land . . .

'The harvest is past, the summer is ended, and we are not saved.'
For the hurt of my poor people I am hurt, I mourn, and dismay has
taken hold of me. Is there no balm in Gilead? Is there no physician
there? Why then has the health of my poor people not been
restored? O that my head were a spring of water, and my eyes a
fountain of tears, so that I might weep day and night for the slain
of my poor people!'

HYMN 363

Let there be peace on earth

'If only we could love the real world,' wrote the theologian Martin
Buber, 'Love it really in its horror, if only we venture to surround
it with the arms of our spirit, our hands will meet hands that grip
them.'

So let us now surround with our prayers those who meet this day
around the table of peace:

O God who hast taught us that all our doings without love are
nothing worth; send down your Holy Spirit, and pour into our
hearts that most excellent gift of love, the very bond of peace and
of all virtues, without which whosoever lives is counted dead before
you; grant this for your only Son Jesus Christ's sake. Amen.

(BCP)

Lord of peace, be with those who are engaged at this present time
in peace talks. Help them to realize that peace comes not through
conquest but through reconciliation; not through winning one's own
way, but through safeguarding the rights of all people. Give the
negotiators the courage to speak frankly and the humility to listen
patiently. Help us all to value peace above victory and justice
above vindictiveness. So may the world become a safer place for us
all, as we learn to trust one another and to live together in peace.
Amen.

Lord, you have said to us 'Peace I leave with you'.
This peace that you give is not that of the world:
it is not the peace of order, when order oppresses;
it is not the peace of silence, when silence is born of suppression;

it is not the peace of resignation, when such resignation is
   unworthy.
Your peace is love for all people,
is justice for all people, is truth for all people,
the truth that liberates and stimulates growth.
Lord, it is this peace we believe in because of your promise.
Grant us peace, and we will give this peace to others. Amen.

(From the Waldensian Liturgy)

Lead me from death to life, from falsehood to truth.
Lead me from despair to hope, from fear to trust.
Lead me from hate to love, from war to peace.
Let peace fill our heart, our world, our universe.
Peace, peace, peace.

(Satish Kumar)

HYMN 367

Put peace into each other's hands

Pollution

New evidence is constantly brought forward in order to suggest that the air of most major cities of the world is filthy. Numerous studies show that deaths from respiratory problems and heart disease increase on days of high pollution. One report in the *British Medical Journal* even suggested that healthy people need not be complacent. In 1995 Britain's chief medical officer admitted for the first time that air pollution could be a killer, rather than simply exacerbating asthma and bronchial disease. Journalist Peter Gruner says: 'One major factor for pollution rests with the diesel engine—especially those of buses, taxis, and heavy goods vehicles.' There are continual suggestions for cities to be freed from the crippling nature of traffic, and some, including Nice, Munich, Rome, and Amsterdam have taken curbing measures.

Traditional Christian prayers from pre-modern, non-technological, unpolluted times speak of continual awe, wonder, and pleasure at God's creation. There is much description of trees, plants, streams, and rivers. There are few, if any, prayers dwelling upon the abuse of and disrespect for nature and animals. The modern world of humankind's plundering and destroying of nature, species, and resources for short-term financial gain is rarely mentioned. However, selfishness and greed are far from unknown; so too is disparity between groups and peoples. Scripture expresses pain and anguish at humankind's folly when it forgets the Creator God, and equally so when it is forgotten that humankind is intended as a co-worker and not an exploiter in the given world. A steady depreciation of the world's resources, knowingly undertaken, is not compatible with an understanding of nature and its attendant world.

HYMN 267

Beauty for brokenness

READING

Job 12.7–10

But ask the animals, and they will teach you; the birds of the air, and they will tell you; ask the plants of the earth, and they will teach you; and the fish of the sea will declare to you. Who among all these does not know that the hand of the Lord has done this? In his hand is the life of every living thing and the breath of every human being.

PRAYERS

As light returns to the world we know,
as flowers open,
as birds sing,
as we rise and see each other
and know we are yet alive here with Jesus,
so we remember creation and give thanks for all life.
Amen.

Good Lord, deliver us
from economic systems that plunder and destroy our planet,
from humankind's assumed right to destroy animals and insects
    under the pretext of progress.

Good Lord, deliver us
from wanton destruction of much beauty,
from uncontrolled use of the seas as a dumping ground,
from polluting the atmosphere.

Good Lord, deliver us
from assuming we are the creators,
from believing all power lies with us,
from ignoring your will and purpose.

HYMN 401

We plough the fields, and scatter

Public Scandal

The personal lives of public figures are frequently exposed to our view when they have been caught in some moral lapse. It is as though their downfall has become a stumbling-block (the literal meaning of the word scandal) for all of us as we endeavour to follow the narrow path of morality. Some of us, whilst deploring the press coverage of such scandals nevertheless find ourselves coming to quick judgements, simply on the basis of what we have read in the media. Rarely do we know the full facts of the situation, nor are we in any position to make such a judgement. We do well to remind ourselves of our own frailties and to seek for others the forgiveness from God which we would claim for ourselves, as we do in our first hymn:

HYMN 20

Praise, my soul, the King of heaven

PRAYER

Almighty God, unto whom all hearts be open, all desires known, and from whom no secrets are hid; Cleanse the thoughts of our hearts by the inspiration of thy Holy Spirit, that we may perfectly love thee, and worthily magnify thy holy Name; through Christ our Lord. Amen.

(BCP)

READING

The Bible reading comes from St John's gospel, though it was probably not actually written by St John. It seems to have been added later by some scribe who wanted to show how graciously Jesus treated even those who were made a public scandal. It is usually placed at the beginning of chapter 8, where Jesus is warning people not to pass judgement on one another. No one except God can really know what is going on in another person's life. It is our own sins we need to submit to scrutiny, not the sins of others. By way of illustration the scribe has added this story of a woman who was caught in the act of adultery and brought to Jesus for judgement.

Early in the morning [Jesus] came again to the temple. All the people came to him and he sat down and began to teach them. The scribes and the Pharisees brought a woman who had been caught in adultery; and making her stand before all of them, they said to him, 'Teacher, this woman was caught in the very act of committing adultery. Now in the law Moses commanded us to stone such women. Now what do you say?' They said this to test him, so that they might have some charge to bring against him. Jesus bent down and wrote with his finger on the ground. When they kept on questioning him, he straightened up and said to them, 'Let anyone among you who is without sin be the first to throw a stone at her.' And once again he bent down and wrote on the ground. When they heard it, they went away, one by one, beginning with the elders; and Jesus was left alone with the woman standing before him. Jesus straightened up and said to her, 'Woman, where are they? Has no one condemned you?' She said, 'No one, sir.' And Jesus said, 'Neither do I condemn you. Go your way, and from now on do not sin again.'

It is tantalizing to wonder what Jesus actually wrote on the ground. Maybe he was just scribbling in the embarrassed silence, or maybe he was spelling out words of grace for a woman who felt disgraced.

HYMN 282 (preferably sung as a solo)

Amazing grace

PRAYER

I thank you, Lord, for knowing me better than I know myself, and for letting me know myself better than others know me. Make me, I pray you, better than they suppose, and forgive what they do not know. Amen.

(Attributed to Abu Bekr, first Calif of Islam)

Most merciful God, deliver us from those sins which cause great hurt to others;
    for all unfaithfulness,
    Lord, forgive us;

for all betrayal of the trust others put in us,
Lord, forgive us;
for every form of self-deception and the way we deceive others,
Lord, forgive us;
for false persuasion of ourselves that we are doing no harm,
Lord, forgive us;
for the sloth which leads us into false compromise,
Lord, forgive us.
Lift us above our failures, Lord. Let your forgiveness restore us and your power remake us through Jesus Christ our Lord. Amen.

We pray for those on whom the glare of publicity falls at this present time. Where there has been wrong-doing, may there be penitence; where there has been hurt, may there be healing; where there has been a betrayal of trust, may there be forgiveness; where there has been a breakdown in relationships, may there be reconciliation. We ask it in the name of the one who neither condemned nor condoned but offered forgiveness, Jesus Christ our Lord. Amen.

God, our Judge, teach us all that we are called to stand as witnesses to your love; not to sit in judgement on those who may deserve your wrath, but to commit them to your mercy for the sake of Jesus Christ our Lord. Amen.

May the merciful God pardon and deliver us from all our sins and make us ministers of grace to others, for the sake of Jesus Christ our Lord. Amen.

HYMN 317

There's a wideness in God's mercy

Racial Violence

The episodes of racial violence that still erupt in our cities from time to time are symptoms of an underlying sickness of the human mind and heart, xenophobia, fear of the stranger. It is a pernicious evil which can cause death to innocent people. In recent decades, it has been seen at its most horrific in the wholesale slaughter of communities in what has been euphemistically called 'ethnic cleansing'. It is a disease that manifests itself daily when people from ethnic minorities are discriminated against, intimidated, or insulted. Such insults are an offence not only to our fellow human beings but to God, the Creator of all humankind. We are all of one kin and therefore are called to be 'kind' to one another, in the literal sense of that word, treating each other as kinsfolk, brothers and sisters with equal claims to justice and respect within the same human family.

HYMN 359

In Christ there is no East or West

READING

In a letter written to communities struggling to work out a way of living together with people of different races and cultures, the writer of the Letter to the Ephesians speaks of the 'new humanity' in Christ, in which there are no longer strangers and aliens, but a recognition of one another as fellow citizens of the Kingdom of God.

Ephesians 2.14

For he is our peace; in his flesh he has made both groups into one and has broken down the dividing wall, that is, the hostility between us. He has abolished the law with its commandments and ordinances, so that he might create in himself one new humanity in place of the two, thus making peace, and might reconcile both groups to God in one body through the cross, thus putting to death that hostility through it. So he came and proclaimed peace to you who were far off, and peace to those who were near; for through him both of us have access in one Spirit to the Father. So then you are no longer strangers and aliens, but you are citizens with the saints and also members of the household of God, built upon the foundation of the apostles and prophets, with Christ Jesus himself as the cornerstone.

PRAYER

Across the barriers that divide race from race:
Reconcile us, O Christ, by your cross.
Across the barriers that divide the rich from the poor:
Reconcile us, O Christ, by your cross.
Across the barriers that divide people of different faiths:
Reconcile us, O Christ, by your cross.
Across the barriers that divide Christians:
Reconcile us, O Christ, by your cross.
Across the barriers that divide men and women, young and old:
Reconcile us, O Christ, by your cross.

(From the St Andrews Press)

AFFIRMATION OF FAITH (from South Africa)

We believe in one God
who created all the world
who will unite all things in Christ
and who wants all people to live together in one family.

We believe in God the Son:
who became human, died and rose in triumph
to reconcile the world to God,
to break down every separating barrier
of race, culture, or class, and to unite all people into one body.
We believe in Jesus Christ:
the only Lord over every area of human life,
who summons everyone: both individual and society,
in both Church and State,
to seek reconciliation and unity between all,
and justice and freedom for all.

We believe in God the Spirit,
the pledge of God's coming reign
who gives the Church power to proclaim the good news to all the
world,
to love and serve all people,
to strive for justice and peace:
to warn that God judges both the individual and the nations;
and to summon all the world to accept
God's reign here and now.

PRAYERS

Let us pray for all who are caught up in racial disturbances, that
violent tempers may be calmed, suspicion allayed, and order
restored.
Nkosi, Nkosi, Lord, have mercy (South Africa)   (*WE* 86)
Let us pray for all who administer justice, that they might do so
without fear or favour, but with wisdom and mercy.
Nkosi, Nkosi, Lord, have mercy.
Let us pray for all who work to bring about right relationships
between the races, that they may counteract all prejudice and at the
same time instil a proper pride that promotes a mutual respect.
Nkosi, Nkosi, Lord, have mercy.
Build us up O Father into the fellowship of the free
that starts in each family and reaches out to the people next door;
that starts in our own community and reaches over barriers of
custom and prejudice to the community on the other side of town,
that starts in our own country and reaches beyond patriotism and
national pride to the nations of the world,
that starts with our own colour and rejoices to claim as brothers and
sisters women and men of every race, for the sake of Jesus Christ
our Lord.

(John Kingsnorth)

Lord Jesus Christ, who stayed to talk with a Samaritan woman, praised the faith of a Syro-Phoenician, and healed the son of a Roman centurion, we thank you for the way our lives are enriched through our encounters with people of different races, other faiths, and many cultures. May we be a blessing to one another, and, coming closer to each other, may we come closer to the God whose love surrounds us all. Amen.

HYMN 104

Christ is alive! Let Christians sing

Rape

Rape is not only a physical violation, it is a desecration of one of God's best gifts to humanity—the gift of being able to express sexually the closest of all loving relationships. In animals, sex is simply a means of procreation; in human beings it is a creative act in itself, expressing the most intimate form of love. Where no love exists and no consent is given, the sexual act is an inhuman violation of the divine purpose and of our human integrity.

A woman who had herself been a victim of rape wrote recently about her experience: 'I know the shame, the humiliation, the rage, the terror, the frustration, the horrible jokes that are made. Alongside the evil and the pain, however, I have known the support of men and women who love me, the unquestioning embrace of those who uphold me, the healing touch of those who rescued me, and the grace of God who sustains me.'

(Janice Love)

HYMN 371

Cradle, O Lord, in your arms everlasting

AFFIRMATION

(From a Rite of Healing from Rape, in *Churches in Solidarity with Women*, WCC 1988)

We love and affirm this our sister who has been hurt. Although she has been injured, she is not destroyed. Although she has been demeaned, she has not lost her integrity. Although she has been subjected to ugliness, yet she is still beautiful. Although evil has gripped her, yet she is still good. We affirm her wholeness, her goodness, her truthfulness, her integrity, her beauty. We dispel the forces of destruction, of ugliness, of violence, which seek to make her their victim.

From violence to her body, **may she be healed.**
From violence to her feelings, **may she be healed.**
From violence to her mind and spirit, **may she be healed.**

READING

The word 'sex' is derived from the word 'secare' which means to cut apart, to divide that which was designed as a whole. The story of creation depicts the harmony in which man and woman, both made in the image of God, celebrated their discovery of one another as being like a discovery of themselves.

Genesis 2.18–24

Then the Lord God said, 'It is not good that the man should be alone; I will make him a helper as his partner' . . . So the Lord God caused a deep sleep to fall upon the man, and he slept; then he took one of his ribs and closed up its place with flesh. And the rib that the Lord God had taken from the man he made into a woman and brought her to the man.
Then the man said,
'This at last is bone of my bones, and flesh of my flesh;
this one shall be called Woman, for out of Man this one was taken.'
Therefore a man leaves his father and his mother and clings to his wife, and they become one flesh. And the man and his wife were both naked, and were not ashamed.

PRAYERS

Praise God, who has created all things and made both man and woman in his own image.

Praise God who has created courtship and marriage, joy and gladness, feasting and laughter, pleasure and delight, love and tenderness, brotherhood and sisterhood, peace and friendship.

Praise God who has sent Jesus Christ to save us from sin and redeem our life from selfishness, and has given us the Holy Spirit to make us one with each other and with God.

God, forgive us that we so often spoil even the best of your gifts to us. Particularly today we confess our shame at the way your gift of sexual pleasure has been abused. Forgive us when we cheapen that gift by the way we talk, the jokes we make, the way we look at one another, the way we use others to gratify our own needs. Teach us how to treat others with reticence, reverence, and respect, until, in mutual commitment and love, we may through our bodies give worship to one another and to you, the source of all love. Amen.

We pray for all those who have suffered bitter experiences and have been victims of violence, rape, abuse:
Lord Jesus Christ, who was moved to anger by the suffering caused to those who were innocent or vulnerable, we bring before you in our prayers women who have been raped, children who have been abused, men who have inflicted pain on one another. Grant your wisdom and compassion to all who deal with both the victims and the perpetrators of sexual offence. Help us all so to reverence one another that we never deface your image in any human being nor cause one of your little ones to stumble. We ask it through your love, given body and soul to redeem our humanity, and make us whole again. Amen.

O God, your generous love surrounds us, and everything we enjoy comes from you. We confess our ingratitude for your goodness and our selfishness in using your gifts. We ask you to forgive us and to fill us with true thankfulness, through Jesus Christ our Saviour. Amen.

May the purpose of God be between us and each purpose, the hand of God between us and each hand, the pain of Christ between us and each pain, the love of Christ between us and each love.

And may the grace of the Lord Jesus Christ, the love of God and the fellowship of the Holy Spirit be with us and with all for whom we have prayed this day. Amen.

HYMN 305

Love divine, all loves excelling

Refugees

There are few more heartbreaking scenes on television than the sight of a long trail of refugees wearily fleeing from some war-ridden zone or famine-stricken land. There are over twenty million of them now, most of them in the poorer countries of the world. Only about one in ten makes it as far as the richer nations of the north, where doors are closing against them. So, to the anguish of having to leave their homes behind, is added the anxiety of not knowing where they can settle, whether they will be allowed to remain and whether they will ever be able to return home again. The experience of exile is a strong biblical theme. The people of Israel, having known for themselves what it was like to be strangers in a foreign land, were frequently reminded of the need to care for the aliens who had come among them. 'You shall not wrong or oppress a resident alien', stated the book of the law, 'for you were aliens in the land of Egypt.'

HYMN 142

Guide me, O thou great Redeemer

PSALM 146

Praise the Lord!
Praise the Lord, O my soul!
I will praise the Lord as long as I live;
I will sing praises to my God all my life long.
Do not put your trust in princes,
in mortals, in whom there is no help.
When their breath departs, they return to the earth;
on that very day their plans perish.
Happy are those whose help is in the God of Jacob,
Whose hope is in the Lord their God,
who made heaven and earth,
the sea, and all that is in them;
who keeps faith for ever;
who executes justice for the oppressed;
who gives food to the hungry.

The Lord sets the prisoners free;
the Lord opens the eyes of the blind.
The Lord lifts up those who are bowed down;
the Lord loves the righteous.
The Lord watches over the strangers;
he upholds the orphan and the widow,
but the way of the wicked he brings to ruin.
The Lord will reign for ever,
your God, O Zion, for all generations.
Praise the Lord!

CHANT

Laudate omnes gentes—praise God, all people (*WE* 93)

PRAYER

God of compassion, we weep with those who long for a place
    they can call their home.
May our tears be not only tears of pity but of charity too.
May our hearts and our hands be open to help them,
And our homelands be ready to receive them.
Laudate omnes gentes
O Lord Christ, who as a boy fled with your parents as a refugee
    to Africa,
have compassion on all refugees in Africa today;
relieve their fear, comfort their distress, and encourage all those
    who have gone to their aid.
Laudate omnes gentes
We pray for all who have been forced to leave their homes.
We think of them on their long journeys.
Keep them safe, and give them the strength to carry on.
Forgive us for our slowness in understanding their need
    and our reluctance to make room for them in our more
    prosperous lands.
Help us to learn from other, poorer countries how to welcome
    the stranger who comes among us.
Laudate omnes gentes
We bring before you, God, those who are anxiously awaiting a

decision as to whether they can stay in the country where they have
sought refuge. May those who judge their case have both wisdom
and generosity of spirit; may those who minister to them during the
waiting time show care and understanding; and wherever they are
finally allowed to settle, grant them your protection and a safe
haven.

Laudate omnes gentes

O bless this people, Lord, who seek their own face
under the mask and can hardly recognize it.
And bless all the peoples of North and South, of East and West,
who sweat blood and tears and sufferings,
and see, in the midst of these millions of waves
the sea swell of the heads of my people,
and grant to them warm hearts that they may clasp
the earth in a girdle of friendly hands,
beneath the rainbow of your peace. Amen.

(WCC RISK book, 1975)

HYMN 348

We are marching in the light of God

A Reunion of Friends

From quiet homes and first beginnings
 Out to the undiscovered ends,
There's nothing worth the wear of winning
But laughter and the love of friends.

(Hilaire Belloc)

The word 'friends' is a fascinating word. It comes originally from an old Germanic root meaning 'free'. William Penn, the founder of the religious community known as the Society of Friends, once wrote, 'There can be no friendship where there is no freedom. Friendship loves a free air, and will not be fenced up in straight and narrow enclosures'. Today we celebrate friendships that have stood the tests of time and of distance. We begin by thanking God for these unbreakable bonds.

HYMN 356

Bind us together, Lord

PRAYER

O God, Friend of us all, we thank you for those whose friendship has enriched our lives in the years that are past. We remember the fun we enjoyed, the fears we shared, the lessons we learned. Though we often dreamed then of what the future might hold for each of us, we come now before you with some dreams unrealized, some plans unfulfilled. But we are grateful to you for the surprises life has brought us and for the support we have known through the love of our friends. Bless this day of reunion, that in remembering the past we may be refreshed to face the future, confident in the love of God which remains constant through all the changing scenes of our lives. Amen.

READING

St Paul depended a lot on his friends. He wrote to the people in Philippi, giving thanks for their friendship and praying for them in words that we can make our own as we pray for our friends:

Philippians 1.3–5, 9–11; 4.4–9

I thank my God every time I remember you, constantly praying
with joy in every one of my prayers for all of you, because of your
sharing in the gospel from the first day until now ... And this is
my prayer, that your love may overflow more and more with
knowledge and full insight to help you to determine what is best, so
that on the day of Christ you may be pure and blameless, having
produced the harvest of righteousness that comes through Jesus
Christ for the glory and praise of God ...

Do not worry about anything, but in everything by prayer and
supplication with thanksgiving let your requests be made known to
God. And the peace of God, which surpasses all understanding,
will guard your hearts and your minds in Christ Jesus. Finally,
beloved, whatever is true, whatever is honourable, whatever is just,
whatever is pure, whatever is pleasing, whatever is commendable, if
there is any excellence and if there is anything worthy of praise,
think about these things. Keep on doing the things that you have
learned and received and heard and seen in me, and the God of
peace will be with you.

SUNG RESPONSE

God of all the world, we have come to give you thanks (Papua
New Guinea)   (*WE* 84)

PRAYERS

We pray first in penitence, asking God to forgive us for our neglect
of old friendships, to enable us to forget old quarrels, to cleanse us
from envy and jealousy, and to save us from all that severs even
our closest relationships.
Lord, in your mercy
Response: **Hear our prayer.**

And we pray in thanksgiving for those true friends who have gone
on loving us in spite of all our faults, who have been a very present
help in times of trouble and who have celebrated with us the joyous
events in our lives. May we never undervalue what their friendship
means to us or fail to keep it in good repair.
Lord in your mercy
Response: **Hear our prayer.**

And we pray in intercession for friends not with us today, whom we name before God as we pray. We think of those who today rejoice over good news, and we share their joy. We think of those who are anxious and have difficult decisions to make, and we pray that they may receive God's guidance and choose the right path. We think of those who are sick and pray that they may have a sense of God's healing presence. And we think of those with whom we have lost touch and pray that in some way, by letter or phone or through the mysterious telepathy of prayer, they may know that they are not forgotten and that their friendship is still valued.
Lord in your mercy
Response: **Hear our prayer.**

And let us remember those of our friends who are no longer with us here on earth but who have gone on into the fuller life beyond. Teach us, Lord, to trust you through life and death, and, though it is hard, to trust you too with the life and death of those who are dear to us. Help us to feel that confidence which comes from believing that you know what is best for them and for us, that in your will we may find our peace. Through Jesus Christ our Lord. Amen.

HYMN 358

Forth in the peace of Christ we go

School-Leaving

L eaving school is a major landmark in most people's lives. It draws to an end the period of life which to all intents and purposes represents pre-adulthood. It signifies responsibilities ahead. The next area may be work, further education or, in much of Western society, a time of deep unsettlement with no full-time employment. People approach their leaving occasion with an attitude largely determined by the immediate future in the categories just mentioned. There are of course those for whom the future is irrelevant, in so far as they desire to remove themselves from schooling. That is their first priority and fulfilment—the rest can or may follow. Leaving occasions do lead to an appraisal of one's life, as determined by that moment. It is positive when a school-leaver can assert self-confidence to handle life, and possesses a strong sense of identity. That person walks into life.

HYMN 39

Tell out, my soul

READING

Ecclesiastes 3.1–8

For everything there is a season, and a time for every matter under heaven:
a time to be born, and a time to die;
a time to plant, and a time to pluck up what is planted;
a time to kill, and a time to heal;
a time to break down, and a time to build up;
a time to weep, and a time to laugh;
a time to mourn, and a time to dance;
a time to throw away stones, and a time to gather stones together;
a time to embrace, and a time to refrain from embracing;
a time to seek, and a time to lose;
a time to keep, and a time to throw away;

a time to tear, and a time to sew;
a time to keep silence, and a time to speak;
a time to love, and a time to hate;
a time for war, and a time for peace.

PRAYER

Let us give thanks to God for the life we have lived so far, and
bring before him the 'ups' and 'downs', our joys and
disappointments, our moments of laughter and those times of tears.
Let us bring to mind those moments . . .
Let us lay before him memories of our school life, whether those
thoughts are positive or negative.
Let us thank God for those people who have been there for us, and
believed in us.
Let us thank God for special friends made during our years of
schooling.
Let us bring to God our fears and worries for the future ahead . . .
Lord, show us what we mean to you and to others.

You invite us to illuminate this world, to find its meaning, and turn
upside down its absurdity. May we dare to do just that.
Amen.

HYMN 351

He who would valiant be

Seafarers

'Those that go down to the sea in ships', wrote the psalmist, 'see the works of the Lord and his wonders in the deep.' Fishermen and sailors are often people of strong faith, as though their constant battle against the elements increases their sense of dependence upon the Lord of wind and waves. John Wesley in his sea journeys was once so impressed by the faith of some of his fellow travellers in the midst of a fearsome storm, that it made him long for a confidence like theirs that could carry him through every kind of tempest. When he eventually found that faith, he expressed it in terms of surviving a storm at sea. In the words of a German hymn he translated, he affirmed:

> Though waves and storms go o'er my head
> Though strength, and health, and friends be gone,
> Though joys be withered all and dead,
> Though every comfort be withdrawn.
> On this my steadfast soul relies—
> Father, Thy mercy never dies!

HYMN 372

Eternal Father, strong to save

PSALM 107.23–32

Some went down to the sea in ships, doing business on the
mighty waters;
they saw the deeds of the Lord, his wondrous works in the deep.
For he commanded and raised the stormy wind, which lifted up
the waves of the sea.
They mounted up to heaven, they went down to the depths.
Their courage melted away in their calamity; they reeled and
staggered like drunkards,
and were at their wits' end.
Then they cried to the Lord in their trouble,
and he brought them out from their distress;

he made the storm be still, and the waves of the sea were
   hushed.
Then they were glad because they had quiet, and he brought them
   to their desired haven.
Let them thank the Lord for his steadfast love
for his wonderful works to humankind.
Let them extol him in the congregation of the people,
and praise him in the assembly of the elders.

PRAYER

A prayer based on John Wesley's personal prayers:

Lord, the winds are often rough, and our own weight presses us
downwards. Reach forth Thy hand, O Lord, Thy saving hand and
speedily deliver us. Fix Thou our steps that we stagger not at the
uneven motions of the world, but steadily go on to our glorious
home, neither censuring our journey by the weather we meet, nor
turning out of the way for anything that befalls us. May Thy Holy
dictates be our map and Thy Holy life be all our guide, and bring
us finally to the quiet harbour of eternal rest. Amen.

READING

One of the best known of all Bible stories is about a storm at sea.
It is the story of Jonah who was trying to escape from God. He felt
that God was calling him to undertake a dangerous mission to the
notoriously wicked city of Nineveh, and he flinched from the fate
that might await him there. So he took a ship going in the opposite
direction. But he was to discover that there is no getting away from
God's purpose for our lives. As another psalmist put it, 'Even
though I take the wings of the morning and dwell in the uttermost
parts of the sea, even there shall thy hand lead me and thy right
hand shall hold me'. It is a tale that has all the salty tang of a
sailor's yarn, but it catches too the savour of a seaman's faith in the
inescapable providence of God. This is how Jonah prayed:

Jonah 2.3–9

Lord, you cast me into the deep, into the heart of the seas, and the
flood surrounded me; all your waves and your billows passed over
me. Then I said, 'I am driven away from your sight; how shall I

look again upon your holy temple?' The waters closed in over me; the deep surrounded me; weeds were wrapped around my head at the roots of the mountains. I went down to the land whose bars closed upon me for ever; yet you brought up my life from the Pit, O Lord my God. As my life was ebbing away, I remembered the Lord; and my prayer came to you, into your holy temple. Those who worship vain idols forsake their true loyalty. But I with the voice of thanksgiving will sacrifice to you; what I have vowed I will pay. Deliverance belongs to the Lord!

PRAYERS

Almighty and eternal God whose way is on the deep, we commend to your care all whose work requires them to go down to the sea in ships. Help them as they battle through the great waters to know your presence with them. Give them courage and cheerfulness, obedience and skill, that they may carry out their duties faithfully, and bring them safely back into harbour where they may earn due reward for all their labours. We ask it for your name's sake. Amen.

And we pray for all who go to the help of those in peril on the sea:

Lord, we pray for all who keep watch and stand ready to go to the aid of those in danger. Keep them alert and vigilant, and help them to be aware of your presence with them, empowering them and encouraging their work of rescue. Give comfort and consolation to all relatives and friends of those who have lost their lives at sea. We ask it in your name. Amen.

Lord, save us from the foolishness of trying to escape from your purpose for our lives. Give us the discernment to hear your voice and the wisdom to obey it. Open wide the windows of our spirits and fill us with your light; open wide the doors of our hearts that we may welcome you with love and receive you with adoration, through Christ our Lord. Amen.

HYMN 321

Will your anchor hold in the storms of life

Into your hands, Lord, we commend all who at this moment are on the high seas. Protect them, speed them on their way, and bring them safely home to those who are waiting to welcome them. We ask it for your name's sake. Amen.

Seasons: Spring

William Thackeray once wrote, 'The rose upon my balcony the morning air perfuming, Was leafless all the winter time and pining for Spring.' William Shakespeare in *King Henry IV* wrote 'Now 'tis the Spring, and weeds are shallow-rooted; Suffer them now and they'll overgrow the garden.'

After a long, cold, and harsh winter, spring is welcomed. The universe seems new-born. Starkness in flower and tree is replaced by a new clothing to delight the senses. Grass grows. Daylight is longer. For the gardener it is a time to check tools and to oil and repair them. For people throwing off thick winter coats and hats there is an eagerness to try new things. Cold foods slowly begin to take over from hot and often heavy meals. But hope and new life, like a new-born child from the womb, are never far from danger, so there is a vulnerability in spring, for cold winds and frosts do return, and bright skies can become dark and heavy with rain.

Spring means Easter. Happy Palm Sunday crowds welcome their King. Later the lowering sky, nails driven into wood, the sight of a cross and a crucified Saviour. Yet there comes resurrection and the empty tomb. The Lord has gone before, announced joyfully by women, and he is encountered by men walking, by people gathering in an upper room, by fishermen bewailing a poor catch. Several Easter hymns, for instance 'Welcome happy morning' and 'Now the green blade riseth', join together creation, nature's rebirth, cross, and resurrection. It was D. H. Lawrence who once complained that the churches sometimes only preach Christ crucified, whereas that is only half the creed, and only half their duty . . . the Apostles' Creed says 'on the third day he rose again'. Lawrence tells the Church that its business is 'to preach Christ born, which is Christmas, Christ crucified, which is Good Friday, and Christ risen, which is Easter, till November and All Saints, and till Annunication, the year belongs to the risen Lord . . . Is the flesh that was crucified become as poison to the crowds in the street, or is it strong blossoming out of the earth's humus?'

HYMN 112

Now the green blade riseth

READINGS

I Corinthians 15.14–15

And if Christ has not been raised, then our proclamation has been in vain and your faith has been in vain. We are even found to be misrepresenting God, because we testified of God that he raised Christ.

Luke 24.2–5

They found the stone rolled away from the tomb, but when they went in, they did not find the body. While they were perplexed about this, suddenly two men in dazzling clothes stood beside them. The women were terrified and bowed their faces to the ground, but the men said to them, 'Why do you look for the living among the dead? He is not here, but has risen.'

PRAYERS

Almighty Father,
you gave your Son to die for us and to rise again
that we may have life in him.
Grant that we may be nourished by his life
and strengthened to serve you in holiness and truth,
through Jesus Christ our Lord.

Almighty Father,
who in your great mercy made the disciples glad
with the sight of the risen Lord,
give us such knowledge of his presence with us
that we may be strengthened and sustained by his risen life
and serve you continually in righteousness and truth,
through Jesus Christ our Lord,
Amen.

HYMN 114

Thine be the glory

Seasons: Summer

HYMN 316

Summer suns are glowing

S ummer means sun. It has warmth. The sea is no longer cold and
forbidding. Waves splash laughter into the eyes of happy
swimmers. Yet the hot sun burns wet skin. Gardens and streets
become oppressive; people are uncomfortable and tired. Plants
wither in the heat, crying for moisture; the street is dusty and its
surface cracks; humans search for shade and long for a breeze.
Sometimes, the sun-worshippers, who had bared all to the rays of
the sun, find their over-exposed skin unbearable.

Summer more than any other time is for being out and about,
perhaps simply to relax and rest, or travel to see some of the sights
and wonders of the world. What can match approaching New York
by the Hudson River after many long days at sea from Britain—or
seeing the Grand Canyon—just smelling and seeing jungle in
Kenya—sitting on the Glazier Express in Switzerland and seeing
such whiteness of snow that eyes cannot easily cope—or standing
on London's Waterloo Bridge and looking towards St Paul's
Cathedral one way, and the Houses of Parliament the other?

But summer and sights, precious as they may be, do not call me
out of my established patterns of life and living. For that I need the
heat and fire of the Gospel. Oddly, summer is bereft of Christian
symbol and celebration. There is almost a standstill between
Pentecost and harvest festival.

READINGS

Luke 23.44

It was now about noon, and darkness came over the whole land
until three in the afternoon, while the sun's light failed.

Revelation 21.22–6

I saw no temple in the city, for its temple is the Lord God the
Almighty and the Lamb. And the city has no need of sun or moon
to shine on it, for the glory of God is its light, and its lamp is the

Lamb. The nations will walk by its light, and the kings of the earth will bring their glory into it. Its gates will never be shut by day—and there will be no night there. People will bring into it the glory and the honour of the nations.

PRAYER

May God become God for us once again.
May we allow him to be for us what he really is.
May we see his true face
instead of the one we give him.

Lord,
Shine the heat of your sun upon our lives.
May the dust and grime of our sins be revealed.
Oh that we would have burning passion and desire!
Oh that in the searing of your love we should become welded,
    transfixed, strong, and sure in the ever present warmth of your
    love!

**Father, we confess that in our thoughts and lives we have often
loved darkness rather than light and sun,
and in the darkness we have betrayed you.**

**Take fire and burn our guilt and hypocrisies,
take water and wash away the blood which we have caused to be
    shed,
take the hot sunlight and dry the tears of those we have hurt,
and heal their wounded souls, minds, and bodies,
take love, and root it in our hearts, transform the dry deserts of
    our prejudices and hatreds,
take our imperfect prayers and purify them
through your strong love.**

Amen.

HYMN 342

Purify my heart

Seasons: Autumn

Louis Savary and Thomas O'Connor suggest a number of things that might be said about autumn. They tell us it is a time when the heart must come face to face with life's predicaments, enlarge its concerns to those of all men and women, accept the challenge to recharge the earth with a new richness, and 'rage against the dying of the light'. So too autumn is the season of the pilgrim soul, the season of love tested and tried, of comfort sought and shared. For many it is harvest time, for the initial sweat, toil, and struggle is over, and the promises of spring now far behind have found their truth. More labour is needed to reap the harvest, but here amidst renewed energy there is the sight of reward, and thankfulness for harvest sown and reaped. For the Hebrews of Old Testament times the cultivating of land was regarded so highly that Yahweh is seen as the founder of husbandry.

It is interesting to note that many harvest hymns go beyond the setting of agriculture and land, for they weave into their message the harvest of the soul. Some hymns carry warning notices! In the seasons of the year, in the Western world, cold, formless winter follows the harvest of autumn—so many hymn writers issue a warning to those who enter the latter part of their lives without due regard for the life they have lived, for heaven may not be their dessert when death comes. In Palestine, ploughing opens the farming season in November after the early rains!

HYMN 397

Come, ye thankful people, come

READING

Isaiah 28.23–9

Listen, and hear my voice;
Pay attention, and hear my speech.
Do those who plough for sowing plough continually?
Do they continually open and harrow their ground?
When they have levelled its surface, do they not scatter dill, sow
    cummin,

and plant wheat in rows
and barley in its proper place,
and spelt as the border?
For they are well instructed;
their God teaches them.

Dill is not threshed with a threshing-sledge,
nor is a cartwheel rolled over cummin;
but dill is beaten out with a stick,
and cummin with a rod.
Grain is crushed for bread,
but one does not thresh it for ever;
one drives a cartwheel and horses over it,
but does not pulverize it.
This also comes from the Lord of hosts;
he is wonderful in counsel,
and excellent in wisdom.

PRAYERS

All our activity will be Amen and Alleluia
There we shall rest and we shall see.
We shall see and we shall love.
We shall love and we shall praise.
Behold what shall be in the end, and shall not end

(St Augustine: *The City of God*)

'Tis the gift to be simple,
'Tis the gift to be free,
'Tis the gift to come down
Where we ought to be.

Lord God,
We come with our lives and lay them before you,
We come at different stages of our lives,
We come asking for forgiveness for time wasted,
We come needing your forgiveness for people exploited,
We come pleading for your forgiveness for love slighted.

Lord Jesus Christ, Son of God, have mercy on me a sinner.

Lord God,
we pray for a good harvest for all peoples who have only known bare fields and barren earth in their lives.

The early Church Father, Irenaeus, said the Kingdom will involve the renewal of the creation: it will be 'restored to its primeval condition' and 'the creation having been renovated and set free, shall fructify with an abundance of all kinds of food, from the dew of heaven, and from the fertility of the earth'.

HYMN 20

Praise, my soul, the King of heaven

Seasons: Winter

In his book, *Curiosities of Popular Customs*, published in 1887, W. S. Walsh wrote:

In England, it is common to hear one say, when the cock crows in the stillness of the November and December nights, 'The cock is crowing for Christmas.' He is supposed to do this for the purpose of scaring off the evil spirits from the holy season.

Perhaps Shakespeare had this in mind when he had Marcellus saying to Horatio and Barnardo in the first act of *Hamlet*:

> Some say that ever 'gainst that season comes
> Wherein our saviour's birth is celebrated
> The bird of dawning singeth all night long;
> And then, they say, no spirit can walk abroad,
> The nights are wholesome; then no planets strike,
> No fairy takes, nor witch hath power to charm,
> So hallowed and so gracious is the time.

HYMN 56

On Christmas night all Christians sing

Certainly, as winter brings its cold draughts to chill the bone, so Advent and Christmas interrupt with their cry that for now squalid acts of havoc and destruction should cease, that 'peace', meaning the cessation of open hostilities, should be observed. For Christmas radiates the word love, and love comes in all seasons, but especially so in the birth of a child in Bethlehem. At Christmas time preachers recall how during the First World War, British and German soldiers climbed out of their trenches. Some sang the famous German carol 'Silent night, holy night'. Soldiers exchanged drinks, pictures of wives and girlfriends, children, brothers and sisters, and yet hours later they were killing each other again.

In its calendar, and certainly in the more ancient carols, the Christian Church has never allowed itself to imagine that evil spirits would depart for long. After all, Boxing Day is the Feast of St

Stephen, the first Christian martyr, and 28 December is Holy Innocents Day or Childermas.

READING

I Maccabees 21.7–12a

Alas! Why was I born to see this,
the ruin of my people, the ruin of the holy city,
and to live there when it was given over to the enemy,
the sanctuary given over to the enemy?
Her temple has become like a person without honour,
her glorious vessels have been carried into exile.
Her infants have been killed in her streets,
her youths by the sword of the foe.
What nation has not inherited her palaces
and has not seized her spoils?
All her adornment has been taken away;
no longer free, she has become a slave.
And see, our holy place, our beauty,
and our glory have been laid waste.

PRAYERS

By the waters of Babylon, there we sat down and wept when we remembered Zion.

Lord God,
winter is a time of waiting.
Our lives are cold and forlorn.
We long for peace in our troubled lives.
Will you come to us?

Shower, O heavens, from above,
and let the skies rain down righteousness.
We are unsettled to the very roots of our being.
Are there precepts to guide us?
How do we behave?—
so we come to you.
Behold, now is the acceptable time;
Behold, now is the day of salvation—
so we come to you.

The people who walked in darkness have seen a great light—his name will be called Wonderful, Counsellor, Mighty God, Everlasting Father, Prince of Peace.
Amen.

HYMN 35

O Come, O Come Emmanuel

Space Exploration

Modern space exploration puts a new gloss on some of the old familiar psalms. The poet, gazing up into the heavens some three thousand years ago, gasped in wonder at the moon and the stars, and went on to ask how God could care also about human life. That could be regarded as a question asked in scorn, as though human beings shrank into insignificance beneath the high, vaulting heavens. But today we marvel at the way the human mind is able to explore even the far reaches of space and to probe the mysteries of the universe. Such astronomical achievements should make us both proud and humble at the same time—proud at all that our human capacity can accomplish, and humble at the awareness of how much more there still is for us to discover about this amazing universe. The great astronomer Kepler displayed that kind of humility when he exclaimed, 'Lord, I am but thinking your thoughts after you!' The more we discover about our universe, the more awesome seems the mystery of its Creator. The poet Joseph Addison expresses that awe in a hymn he wrote three hundred years ago:

HYMN 28

The spacious firmament on high

PSALM 8

O Lord, our Sovereign, how majestic is your name in all the earth!
You have set your glory above the heavens.
Out of the mouths of babes and infants you have founded a bulwark because of your foes,
to silence the enemy and the avenger.
When I look at your heavens, the work of your fingers,
the moon and the stars that you have established;
what are human beings that you are mindful of them,
mortals that you care for them?
Yet you have made them a little lower than God,
and crowned them with glory and honour.
You have given them dominion over the works of your hands;

you have put all things under their feet,
all sheep and oxen,
and also the beasts of the field,
the birds of the air, and the fish of the sea,
whatever passes along the paths of the seas.
O Lord, our Sovereign,
how majestic is your name in all the earth!

ACCLAMATION

Heaven is singing for joy, Alleluia!   (Argentina)   (*WE* 28)

PRAYER

Lord of the universe, as we explore your heavens, may we magnify your name. When you visited our earth, you magnified us by becoming one of us. You have shown us how mindful you are of us. Forgive us that so often we fall far lower than the angels. May all our works be crowned with glory and honour, for your name's sake. Amen.

> Creator God, we praise you for all that we are learning through the work of astronomers and astronauts about the nature of our universe.
> We are discovering how small our world is, a tiny speck in the whole canopy of the heavens.
> **May its very fragility strengthen our resolve to care for our planet as good stewards of your creation.**
> We are discovering how vast the heavens are, out-reaching our measurements of time or space.
> **May the limits of our knowledge increase our awareness of an eternal reality that lies beyond all our powers of imagining.**
> We are discovering how complex is the design of your universe, with its interdependent galaxies.
> **May our dependence upon the sun and the moon deepen our sense of being one world, turning through day and night, as light dawns from land to land.**
> We are discovering how mysterious are all your works and how hidden are your purposes.

May we learn through the wonders of space exploration to marvel at all the human mind can achieve and to acknowledge all that we still do not understand.

God of our universe, we pray for all space-travellers who continue to probe the secrets of the skies. Grant them protection, courage, and wisdom, and bring them safely down to earth again. We believe this earth to be a place which you have blessed through the presence of Jesus among us. May his spirit guide us as we reach out to other planets, that all our journeys may be made in peace and in accordance with your purposes for the whole of creation.

HYMN 10

Immortal, invisible, God only wise

Sports Spectators

The spectators are among the most important participants in any sports event. Every stadium bears evidence of that. As the supporters crowd into the stands, the excitement mounts long before the game begins. The fortunes of the competing teams can be determined, not solely by the skill of the players, but by the extent of the crowd's encouragement of their effort. Success is made all the sweeter by the applause of those who feel they have a share in the victory, whilst the bitterness of defeat can depress a whole community. The game played by the few belongs to the many.

READING

The writer to the Hebrews uses the image of the sports arena as a mirror of life itself. We are all, as it were, players in a game which is being watched by a great host of spectators whose presence can encourage us even when the going gets tough.

Hebrews 12.1–2

Therefore, since we are surrounded by so great a cloud of witnesses, let us also lay aside every weight and the sin that clings so closely, and let us run with perseverance the race that is set before us, looking to Jesus the pioneer and perfecter of our faith.

That same sense of an encouraging host surrounding us is expressed in the song sung often at football matches:

HYMN 320

When you walk through a storm

PRAYER

God of our life, we thank you for all the extra enjoyment we find in life through sport. We rejoice in the skill and the strength of men and women who through training and discipline have reached the peak of great achievement. We pray that we too through determination and commitment may make the best of whatever talents you have given us.

Response: **Those who wait on the Lord shall renew their strength.**

We thank you for those whose encouragement enables us to mount up with wings as eagles, to run and not be weary, to walk and not faint. Help us in our turn to give the encouraging word to those who feel they are not winning through, or who have ceased to make any real effort.

Those who wait on the Lord shall renew their strength.

We pray for all those for whom sport has become a means of livelihood. May the pressures not be too great, nor the rewards too corrupting. May they continue to find joy in their game and satisfaction in knowing the pleasure they give to others.

Those who wait on the Lord shall renew their strength.

We pray for all team supporters, that they may show loyalty that does not depend on success, rivalry that does not erupt into hatred, enthusiasm that does not exceed the bounds of good behaviour, so that everyone may enjoy your good gift of friendly competition.

Those who wait on the Lord shall renew their strength.

READING

St Paul seems to have admired athletes and used their dedication and discipline as an example of the way we should live our lives.

I Corinthians 91.24–7

Do you not know that in a race the runners all compete, but only one receives the prize? Run in such a way that you may win it. Athletes exercise self-control in all things; they do it to receive a perishable garland; but we an imperishable one. So I do not run aimlessly nor do I box as though beating the air; but I punish my body and enslave it, so that after proclaiming to others I myself should not be disqualified.

And right at the end of his life, in his second letter to Timothy, Paul returns to the same theme:

2 Timothy 4.7–8

I have fought the good fight, I have finished the race, I have kept the faith. From now on there is reserved for me the crown of righteousness, which the Lord, the righteous judge, will give to me on that day, and not only to me but also to all who have longed for his appearing.

PRAYER

Lord, help me to follow the course you have set before me, to run a straight race and to keep going until the end. Keep me aware of the great company of your saints who cheer me on, and grant that I in my turn may encourage those to whom I will pass on the baton of faith.

And may he who was there with us at the beginning of the race be with us at its end through Jesus Christ our Lord. Amen.

HYMN 290

Fight the good fight with all thy might

Taizé

Religious periodicals, church leaders planning spiritual renewal for their young people, and worship committees cannot let a year pass without reference to Taizé.

Taizé is a tiny village in Burgundy. Its nearest neighbour is Cluny. It was here that in 1940 a young Swiss, Roger Schutz-Marsauche, purchased property. His dream was to establish a community that would have at the forefront of its existence Christ and the Gospel. Its way of life, its outreach, would be a sign, a parable of the reconciliation which God wills for his people. The Second World War caused a slight hiccup to his plans and vision. But in 1944 the community came back to Taizé and in 1949 seven brothers took solemn vows. Although at first the community drew its support from churches of the Reformation, denominational labels have now ceased to be of concern. The community wishes to emphasize unity amongst Christian believers. By the mid-1990s there were 100 brothers, and at any one time as many as 6,000 pilgrims from all the continents of the world. Each year a European meeting is attended by young adults for six days. Worship is at the heart of the Taizé community. Its liturgical settings and music have gained world-wide popularity. Each weekend, from Friday evening to the Eucharist on Sunday, the Easter celebration is observed.

Simplicity is one of its benchmarks. Joy is common to its deliberations. Taizé, unlike some modern religious developments, offers no membership, no special advantages, no monetary appeals. Its mission is simple: that people should see the Lord.

HYMN 214

Bless the Lord, my soul

READING

Psalm 100

Make a joyful noise to the Lord, all the earth,
Worship the Lord with gladness;
come into his presence with singing.

Know that the Lord is God.
It is he that made us, and we are his;
we are his people, and the sheep of his pasture.

Enter his gates with thanksgiving,
and his courts with praise.
Give thanks to him, bless his name.

For the Lord is good;
his steadfast love endures for ever,
and his faithfulness to all generations.

PRAYERS

Lord

we thank you for the grace of Taizé, for its message of
  reconciliation;

we thank you for the vision of its founder and the continuing
  commitment of its brothers;

we thank you for its world-wide gathering;

we thank you for its worship, its music, the disarming simplicity of
  words and tunes;

we thank you that in an age of restlessness, uncertainty, and doubt,
  Taizé is a place where young people come, respect, and are
  blessed;

we thank you that Christians can come to Taizé and share their
  differences openly,

yet we ask your forgiveness that some of the historic divisions of
  Christendom are evidenced at Taizé;

we ask for your forgiveness that the Lord's Supper is still a point
  where unity is not seen.

Father,

we also pray for other gatherings of Christians that take place. In
Britain we pray for the Iona Community, for Greenbelt, Spring
Harvest, Easter People, and for [name]. We thank you for their
work.

We invite others here with us from other countries to ask us to
pray for similar gatherings [name].

HYMN 240

O Lord, hear my prayer

Travel Accidents

Travel is such a normal part of life these days that news of an accident—an air crash, a rail disaster, a car collision, comes as a shock to us all. Our first thought is to wonder whether anyone we know personally is involved. Whether that is so or not, we realize that there are people somewhere whose lives have been convulsed by this event and who have been plunged into sudden grief. Our prayers go out in sympathy to those who have been bereaved, injured, or affected in any way. The fact that such an accident hits our headlines and sends a shudder through us all is a reminder in itself of how much we take safe travel for granted. Every day thousands of planes cross the airways of the world and land safely without that fact being considered newsworthy. Trains, once regarded as threatening monsters, speed easily along their tracks across the continents. The car, which a century ago was still thought of as a marvel, is today one of our main means of transport. We do not expect accidents. They have become extraordinary events. So we begin our worship by praising the God who has taken the risk of entrusting such power to human beings that we live dangerously, but always ultimately under God's protection.

HYMN 281

All my hope on God is founded

PRAYER

God of all power, we acknowledge the trust you have put in us by enabling men and women to unlock some of the secrets of power. Keep us aware of the limits of our knowledge and the extent of our responsibility to use your gifts wisely and with reverence, for your name's sake. Amen.

READING

Though we may not know the names of the people who are suffering as a result of this accident, we are assured that each of them is known by name to God, who cares for us with an intimate love that is concerned with every detail of our lives.

Luke 12.4–7

'I tell you, my friends, do not fear those who kill the body, and after that can do nothing more. But I will warn you whom to fear: fear him who, after he has killed, has authority to cast into hell. Yes, I tell you, fear him! Are not five sparrows sold for two pennies? Yet not one of them is forgotten in God's sight. But even the hairs of your head are all counted. Do not be afraid; you are of more value than many sparrows.'

PSALM (verses from Psalm 139)

Where can I go from your spirit?
Or where can I flee from your presence?
If I ascend to heaven, you are there;
if I make my bed in Sheol, you are there.
If I take the wings of the morning and settle at the farthest limits
    of the sea,
even there your hand shall lead me,
and your right hand shall hold me fast.
If I say, 'Surely darkness shall cover me,
and the light around me become night',
even the darkness is not dark for you;
the night is as bright as the day,
for darkness is as light to you.

PRAYERS

O God, who looks on the whole world as though it were a single soul and upon each single soul as though it were the whole world, look with pity upon all whose world has become dark today. Visit with your comforting presence each stricken home so that sorrow shall not overwhelm your children nor grief drive them far from you. May the love they receive from others illuminate their darkness and may the hands stretched out to help hold them fast, for your sake.
In your mercy, **hear our prayer.**

God of compassion, we pray for all those in the emergency services who have gone to the scene of this accident. May their professional skills keep them confident and calm in the face of suffering and may their presence bring reassurance to those to whom they minister.
In your mercy, **hear our prayer.**

God of truth, we pray for those who will be investigating the causes of this disaster. May nothing be hidden that should be revealed and may lessons be learned which can prevent such a tragedy from happening again.
In your mercy, **hear our prayer.**

God of mercy, we pray for those who carry any responsibility for what has happened. May they be saved from unremitting remorse. If they were in error, correct them; if they were careless, teach them to care; if they were the victims of circumstance beyond their control, restore their confidence, and may they know that whatever the fault, you can forgive those who are truly sorry.
In your mercy, **hear our prayer.**

Gracious God, we commend to your keeping all who travel by air or sea, by rail or road. Go with them on their journey, protect them by your presence, direct them in the ways of courtesy and concern for others, and bring them safely to their destination, for your name's sake. Amen.

TEN COMMANDMENTS FOR DRIVERS

1. You shall have no other aim than to protect the sanctity of human life.
2. You shall not be obsessed by the power of your vehicle nor the speed of your driving nor the urgency of your business, for neither power nor speed nor business is as important as safety.
3. You shall not swear nor make angry gestures at other drivers lest your anger intimidate them.
4. Remember to allow periods of rest during long journeys. Tiredness can kill.
5. Honour all pedestrians and cyclists that their days may be long on the road you share.

6. You shall not drink and drive lest you cause death on the roads.
7. You shall not engage in distracting phone conversations whilst driving.
8. You shall not steal parking space that is not lawfully yours.
9. You shall not give false witness about any accident you have seen or caused.
10. You shall not covet your neighbour's speed, nor overtake aggressively, but, for God's sake, treat all fellow travellers with courtesy and consideration.

Lord, incline our hearts to keep these laws.

> Alone with none but thee, my God,
> I journey on my way.
> What need I fear, when thou art near
> O King of night and day?
> More safe am I within thy hand
> Than if a host did round me stand. Amen.

(St Columba)

HYMN 340

One more step along the world I go

At a Time of Uncertainty

It is always unsettling when we are having to wait while some decision is made which could affect the whole course of future events. That is true whether it applies to a nation awaiting the outcome of an election, or when personally we are faced with having to make a decision which could change the pattern of the rest of our lives. Even those of us who firmly believe that ultimately, when we look back, we can trace the guidance of God in the course of events, nevertheless find it difficult looking ahead to discern any clear direction or to know exactly which path to take. Yet there remains the feeling that somewhere, somehow, God is watching over us.

PRAYER

Lord of all history, we believe that it is not only from a distance that you rule over the affairs of peoples and nations, but that you yourself have entered our history to show us all that humanity could become if we followed your way, trusted in your truth, and committed our lives into your hands. Save us from restless anxiety and endless speculation, and help us to live in the immediate moment, taking each step as it comes, believing that you will guide us safely to our journey's end, through Jesus Christ our Lord.

One of the effects of uncertainty in our national life is that those who follow the news closely keep making predictions about what is likely to happen next. As each news story breaks, the political correspondents and the leader writers become instant prophets, drawing on their vast knowledge of both the past and the present as they spell out for us the possible future. But then so often a surprise element comes into the story and the predictions have to be reassessed. That is true in our personal histories too. We often think we have our lives well mapped out, and then some unexpected event intervenes and the whole scenario is changed. It is almost as though we are characters in a novel, being written by an author who lets us have our own way much of the time, but keeps his hand firmly on the final outcome of the plot.

That personal trust in the continuing guidance of God is expressed in the popular hymn:

HYMN 174

God is working his purpose out

The psalmist takes this trust in God's guidance even further. He believes God holds the destiny of all the nations in his hands, an idea expressed in Psalm 33, beginnng to read at verse 6:

PSALM (read responsively or chanted)

By the word of the Lord the heavens were made,
and all their host by the breath of his mouth.
He gathered the waters of the sea as in a bottle;
he put the deeps in storehouses.
Let all the earth fear the Lord;
let all the inhabitants of the world stand in awe of him.
For he spoke, and it came to be
he commanded, and it stood firm.
The Lord brings the counsel of the nations to nothing;
he frustrates the plans of the peoples.
The counsel of the Lord stands for ever,
the thoughts of his heart to all generations.

PRAYER

Help us, O God, to understand what your will is in the confusion and unrest of our times. Give us insight to distinguish between the signs of your Spirit demanding change and renewal, and the signs of human greed and lust for power, that we may be your fellow workers in creating an order of society which acknowledges your sovereign love and confers dignity on all your people. Amen.

(NEM p. 68)

INTERCESSIONS

We pray, Lord, for all who have difficult decisions to make at this time:
(The following biddings to be read by different voices)

For Members of Parliament on whom rests the responsibility of
enacting legislation;
Response: **Lord, hear our prayer.**
For members of juries who this day will be giving their verdicts
on those accused of offending against the law;
Lord, hear our prayer.
For those conducting interviews which will decisively affect the
future of their candidates;
Lord, hear our prayer.
For Church leaders, and particularly for those who meet in
council together across the denominations;
Lord, hear our prayer.
For all who personally face decisions about their work, their
marriages, their homes, their children's future, the care of the
elderly, their own health;
Lord, hear our prayer.

Father, teach us not only what your will is, but how to do it. Teach
us the best way of doing the best thing, lest we spoil the end by
unworthy means.

(J. H. Jowett)

God of all grace, give to us and to all your people, in times of
anxiety, serenity, in times of hardship, courage, in times of
uncertainty, patience, in times of sorrow, comfort, and at all times
a quiet trust in your wisdom and love, and may the blessing of God
the Father, the Son and the Holy Spirit be with us all now and for
evermore. Amen.

(*NEM* 101)

HYMN 179
Thy hand, O God, has guided

Unity in Song

For many people, modern technology, communication systems, and global marketing have reduced humankind to one great family. Music has been at the forefront of this unity of races, colours, languages, and religions.

It was in 1967 that 400 million people watched the Beatles record *All You Need Is Love* in Studio One at the famous Abbey Road studios in London. It was telecast 'live' via satellite to twenty-six nations around the world as part of a six-hour television programme, *Our World*, itself part of the Canadian Expo '67. Nearly twenty years later, in 1986, there was Live Aid. Later came the Mandela concert to celebrate both the release from prison and the greatness of Nelson Mandela. The World Cup football competition in 1990 was serenaded in song by Pavarotti, and as a by-product millions discovered opera and classical music. The Rugby World Cup took as its theme *World in Union* performed by New Zealand opera singer Kiri Te Kanawa. A BBC television programme, *Songs of Praise*, has brought together the peoples of Coventry and Dresden, two cities much affected by bombing and destruction in the Second World War. Christians from former Iron Curtain countries have been seen celebrating their freedom to worship and give praise.

Music's ability to unite and bring people together is surely one reason why the Scriptures, when they tell people to worship the Lord, suggest it is done in music.

HYMN 219

Father, we love you

READINGS

Psalm 147.1–3

> Praise the Lord!
> How good it is to sing praises to our God;
> for he is gracious, and a song of praise is fitting.
> The Lord builds up Jerusalem;

he gathers the outcasts of Israel.
He heals the broken-hearted,
and binds up their wounds.

Psalm 149.1, 3–6a, 9b

Praise the Lord!
Sing to the Lord a new song,
his praise in the assembly of the faithful.
Let them praise his name with dancing,
making melody to him with tambourine and lyre.
For the Lord takes pleasure in his people;
he adorns the humble with victory.
Let the faithful exalt in glory;
let them sing for joy on their couches.
Let the high praises of God be in their throats.
This is glory for all his faithful ones.
Praise the Lord!

PRAYER

We give thanks for the varied and joyful nature of humankind.
We give thanks for the races, colours, languages, experiences, and
traditions of humankind.
We give thanks for times when the peoples of the world come
together in peace and celebration.
We give thanks for music in its multiplicity of forms.
Tell out my soul, the greatness of the Lord,
Rejoice my spirit, in God my saviour.

HYMN 248

Sing of the Lord's goodness

Volcano

There can be no sight more awesome than that of a volcano in full eruption. Even a slumbering mountain has its own majestic mystery, but when that huge mass explodes, it must seem as though some great monster is threatening to engulf the earth. Chaos threatens a world of order; a fatal flaw has cracked open in the design of creation. To whom can men and women turn for reassurance? When all else is shaken, the psalmist expresses an unshakeable faith that there is still order at the heart of the universe, and that despite the flaw in its fabric the creation is still under the control of its Creator. 'God is our refuge and strength,' he declares, 'a very present help in time of trouble. Therefore will we not fear though the earth be removed and though the mountains be carried into the midst of the sea.'

HYMN 336

Oft in danger, oft in woe

PRAYER

God our maker, this world you have created is full of mystery. We marvel at its grandeur and beauty; we tremble before its energy and power. We confess in humility that we have learned to control neither the tumultuous forces of nature nor the tumult within our own hearts. We ask you to give protection to those who live under the shadow of great mountains, and in this time of tumult to provide those in peril with shelter and comfort. Strengthen all who go to their aid and sustain them by a faith based on the sure foundation of your love undergirding the whole universe. Amen.

PSALM 46

God is our refuge and strength,
a very present help in trouble.
Therefore we will not fear, though the earth should change,
though the mountains shake in the heart of the sea;
though its waters roar and foam,

though the mountains tremble with its tumult.
There is a river whose streams make glad the city of God,
the holy habitation of the Most High.
God is in the midst of the city; it shall not be moved;
God will help it when the morning dawns.
The nations are in an uproar, the kingdoms totter;
he utters his voice, the earth melts.
The Lord of hosts is with us;
the God of Jacob is our refuge.

READING

In the New Testament there is a vivid description of what must
have been something similar to a volcano on Mount Sinai, which
filled people with dread. But the writer to the Hebrews reminds
them that God speaks to us not in the threats of thunder but in the
promise of everlasting mercy. The very fragility of our temporal
world should urge us to set our minds on the stability of God's
eternal kingdom.

Hebrews 12.18–29

You have not come to something that can be touched, a blazing
fire, and darkness, and gloom, and a tempest, and the sound of a
trumpet, and a voice whose words made the hearers beg that not
another word be spoken to them. (For they could not endure the
order that was given, 'If even an animal touches the mountain, it
shall be stoned to death.' Indeed, so terrifying was the sight that
Moses said, 'I tremble with fear.') But you have come to Mount
Zion, and to the city of the living God, the heavenly Jerusalem,
and to innumerable angels in festal gathering, and to the assembly
of the firstborn who are enrolled in heaven, and to God the judge
of all, and to the spirits of the righteous made perfect, and to
Jesus, the mediator of a new covenant, and to the sprinkled blood
that speaks a better word than the blood of Abel.

See that you do not refuse the one who is speaking; for if they did
not escape when they refused the one who warned them on earth,
how much less will we escape if we reject the one who warns from
heaven! At that time his voice shook the earth; but now he has
promised, 'Yet once more I will shake not only the earth but also

the heavens.' This phrase 'Yet once more' indicates the removal of what is shaken—that is, created things—so that what cannot be shaken may remain. Therefore, since we are receiving a kingdom that cannot be shaken, let us give thanks, by which we offer to God an acceptable worship with reverence and awe; for indeed our God is a consuming fire.

Response:

Giver of life, sustain your creation (Taiwan) (*WE* 116)

PRAYERS

Lord, we are a flawed people and we live in a flawed world, yet we believe your purposes in creation were good. So, when our world is shaken and homes are destroyed, and lands devastated, we plead for your mercy. When we are tempted to despair, grant us a new vision of your glory, high above the mountains, giving us courage and strength to face all the challenges of our environment and struggle against every hardship with unshaken faith. Amen.

Thomas Hardy once wrote:
'The human race is to be seen as one great network of tissue which quivers when one part is shaken, like a spider's web if touched.'
Lord, our nerves quiver as we realize how vulnerable human life is. We pray for all whose lives have been suddenly overturned by the eruption of events for which they were unprepared. Arm them with the courage of faith, the serenity of hope, and the enduring power of love which can cast out all fear, for your name's sake. Amen.

May the peace of God, which passes all understanding, keep our hearts and minds in the knowledge and love of God, and may mercy, peace, and love be with us all evermore. Amen.

HYMN 6

God moves in a mysterious way

War

'The war was not strife. It was murder,' wrote D. H. Lawrence of the First World War, 'each side trying to murder the other side evilly.' Yet war has continued to be a major feature of our modern world. Since the end of the Second World War, over twenty million people have died through warfare, the majority of them civilians. It is estimated that there are now some twenty-seven million people displaced as a result of local wars. The arms trade is among the world's most lucrative global enterprises. 'My greatest weapon', said Mahatma Gandhi, 'is prayer.' So today we turn to prayer for those caught up in the present conflicts across the world.

HYMN 379

God! As with silent hearts we bring to mind

PRAYER

To you, Creator of nature and humanity, of truth and beauty, I pray:

Hear my voice, for it is the voice of the victims of all wars and violence among individuals and nations.

Hear my voice, for it is the voice of all children who suffer and will suffer when people put their faith in weapons and war.

Hear my voice when I beg you to instil into the hearts of all human beings the wisdom of peace, the strength of justice, and the joy of fellowship.

Hear my voice, for I speak for the multitudes in every country and in every period of history, who do not want war and are ready to walk the way of peace.

Hear my voice and grant insight and strength so that we may always respond to hatred with love, to injustice with total dedication to justice, to need with the sharing of self, to war with peace.

O God, hear my voice, and grant unto the world your everlasting peace.

(Pope John Paul II, quoted in *Prayers for Peace* 9)

READING

God's promise to the world given through the prophet's vision.

Micah 4.1–4

In days to come the mountain of the Lord's house shall be established as the highest of the mountains, and shall be raised up above the hills. Peoples shall stream to it, and many nations shall come and say: 'Come, let us go up to the mountain of the Lord, to the house of the God of Jacob; that he may teach us his ways and we may walk in his paths.' For out of Zion shall go forth instruction, and the word of the Lord from Jerusalem. He shall judge between many peoples, and shall arbitrate between strong nations far away; they shall beat their swords into ploughshares, and their spears into pruning-hooks; nation shall not lift up sword against nation, neither shall they learn war any more; but they shall all sit under their own vines and under their own fig trees, and no one shall make them afraid; for the mouth of the Lord of hosts has spoken.

PRAYER

O God of many names,
Lover of all nations
We pray for peace.
Peace in [name],
Peace in [name],
Peace in the world.
The peace of your will,
The peace of our need.

INTERCESSIONS

For all who are bearing the brunt of battle, in the armed forces
and among innocent civilians, Lord hear our prayer.
Dona nobis pacem—Give to us peace.
For all who are anxious, separated far from those they love,
Lord hear our prayer.
Dona nobis pacem.
For all who have been bereaved through battle, Lord hear our
prayer.

Dona nobis pacem.

On all who have been taken prisoner, Lord have mercy.

Christ, have mercy.

On all who are wounded and in pain, Lord have mercy.

Christ, have mercy.

On all who must take command and put human lives at risk,
Lord have mercy.

Christ, have mercy.

For all who seek to negotiate a peaceful solution of conflict, Lord
in your mercy

Hear our prayer.

For all who minister to the wounded, the homeless, the destitute,
Lord in your mercy

Hear our prayer.

For all who strive to turn the weapons of war into the tools of
peace, Lord in your mercy

Hear our prayer.

> Light looked down and beheld Darkness,
> 'Thither will I go', said Light.
> Peace looked down and beheld War,
> 'Thither will I go', said Peace.
> Love looked down and beheld Hatred.
> 'Thither will I go', said Love.
> So came Light and shone;
> So came Peace and gave Rest
> So came Love and gave Life,
> And the Word was made flesh and dwelt among us.
>
> (Laurence Housman)

'Peace I leave with you,' said Jesus, 'my own peace such as the
world cannot give. Set your troubled hearts at rest, and banish your
fears.' Amen.

'Neither shall they learn war any more,' said the prophet. The old
spiritual expresses the same hope in the words, 'I'm gonna study
war no more'.

HYMN 24

Thy kingdom come, O God

Resource Material

This is a source guide and not an attempt to list an exhaustive, far-reaching coverage of material. Obviously other subject areas could have been covered, including 'prose' and 'music' but there is a limit to a general guide, and both of these areas are extensive. A stamped addressed envelope should be enclosed when corresponding with organizations listed in the section headed *Useful Addresses*.

USEFUL ADDRESSES

Information may be obtained from these organizations. This can give extra input to the main material found in this book.

Afro-Caribbean Educational Resource Project, Centre for Learning Resources, 275 Kennington Lane, London SE11 5QZ.

Alliance Music, PO Box 410, Aylesbury, Bucks HP17 8YU.

Amnesty International, 99–111 Rosebery Avenue, London EC1R 4RE.

Animal Welfare Trust, 143 Charing Cross Road, London WC2.

Articles of Faith Ltd, Resource House, Kay Street, Bury BL9 6BU.

Argus Communications, DLM House, Edinburgh Way, Harlow, Essex CM20 2HL.

Arts Centre Group, St Peter's Church, Vere Street, London W1.

Association of Mouth and Foot Painting Artists, 9 Inverness Place, London W2.

Baptist Union, PO Box 44, 129 Broadway, Didcot, Oxfordshire OX11 8RT.

BBC Education Information, White City, London W12 7RS.

BBC Radio, Broadcasting House, Portland Place, London W1.

BBC Radiovision, BBC Enterprises, Villiers House, The Broadway, London W5.

BBC Television Centre, Wood Lane, London W12 7TS.

Beauty Without Cruelty, 40 Marylebone High Street, London W1.

Bible Reading Fellowship, Peter's Way, Sandy Lane West, Oxford, OX4 5HG.

Bible Society, Stonehill Green, Westlea, Swindon SN5 7DG.

Boys' Brigade, The, Felden Lodge, Hemel Hempstead, Herts HP3 0BL.

Buddhist Society, 58 Ecclestone Square, London SW1V 1PH.

Campaign Against The Arms Trade, 11 Goodwin Street, Finsbury Park, London N4 3HQ.

Campaigners, Campaigners House, St Mark's Close, Colney Heath, St Albans, Herts AL4 0NQ.

Cassell, Geoffrey Chapman & Mowbray, Wellington House, 125 Strand, London WC2R 0BB.

Catholic Fund for Overseas Development, 21a Soho Square, London W1V 6NR.

Catholic Youth Service Council, 41 Cromwell Road, London SW7 2DH.

CEM in Scotland, St Colm's Education Centre, 20 Inverleith Terrace, Edinburgh EH3 5NS.

Centre for Urban Educational Studies, 34 Aberdeen Park, London N5.

Christian Aid Educational Department, PO Box 100, London SE1 7RT.

Christian Education Movement, Royal Buildings, Victoria Street, Derby DE1 1GW.

Christian Resources Exhibitions, 2 Forge House, Summerleys Road, Princes Risborough, Bucks HP27 9DT.

Christian World Centre, 123 Deansgate, Manchester M60 1SD.

Christian Youth Fellowship Association, 32 Fleet Street, London EC4Y 1DB.

Christians Against Racism and Fascism, BM Box 8474, London WC1N 3XX.

Churches' Child Protection Advisory Agency, PCCA, PO Box 133, Swanley, Kent BR8 7UQ.

Church Information Office, Church House, Deans Yard, London SW1P 3NZ.

Church Missionary Society, 157 Waterloo Road, London SE1 8UU.

Clear Vision Trust, Buddhist Educational Charity, 16–20 Turner Street, Manchester M4 1DZ.

Commission for Racial Equality, Education Office, Elliott House, 10/12 Allington St, London SE1E 5EH.

Christian Impact, St Peter's Church, Vere Street, London W1.

Christian Performers, Directory of, 236 Sebert Road, London E7.

Christians In Caring Professions, King's House, 175 Wokingham Road, Reading, Berks RG6 1LT.

Church of Scotland, Board of Social Responsibility, Charis House, 47 Milton Road East, Edinburgh EH15 2SR.

Church of Scotland Video, 22 Colinton Road, Edinburgh EH10 5EQ.

Commonweath Institute, Kensington High Street, London SW1E.

Community Service Volunteers, Advisory Service, 237 Pentonville Road, London N1 9NJ.

Concordia Video and Film Council Ltd, 201 Felixstowe Road, Ipswich, Suffolk IP3 9BJ.

Corrymeela Community, PO Box 118, Reading RG1 1SL.

Council of Christians and Jews, 1 Dennington Park Road, West End Lane, London NW6 1AX.

Council of Churches for Britain and Ireland, 35–41 Lower Marsh Street, London SE1 7RL.

Council for Nature, Zoological Gardens, Regents Park, London NW1.

Council for the Protection of Rural England, 4 Hobart Place, London SW1.

CTVC Video, Hillside Studios, Merry Hill Road, Bushey, Watford WD2 1DR.

Department of Education and Youth of the Reform Synagogues of Great Britain, Manor House, 80 East End Road, Finchley, London N3 25Y.

Barnardo's, Tanner's Lane, Barkingside, Olford, Essex.

Easter People, Raynes Park Methodist Church, Tolverne Road, London SW20 0TJ.

Ecology Party, 104 South Hill Park, London NW3.

Elmhurst Centre for Continuing Education, Newton Road, Chapeltown, Leeds LS7 4HE.

Epworth Review, Methodist Publishing House, Ivatt Way, Peterborough PE3 7PG.

European Theological Media, PO Box 777, Carlisle CA3 0QS.

Equity, Guild House, Upper St Martin's Lane, London WC2H 9EG.

Evangelical Alliance, Whitefield House, 186 Kennington Park Road, London SE11 4BT.

Falmer Press, Rankine Road, Basingstoke, Hants RG24 8PR.

Family Planning Association (Education Unit), 27–35 Mortimer Street, London W1.

Free Church Federal Council, 86 Tavistock Place, London WC1H 9RT.

Friends of the Earth, 377 City Road, London EC1.

Frontier Youth Trust, 130 City Road, London EC1V 2NJ.

Genesis Arts, 6 Broadcourt, Covent Garden, London WC2.

Girl Guides Association, 17–19 Buckingham Palace Road, London SW1.

Girls' Brigade, Foxhall Road, Didcot, Oxfordshire OX11 7BQ.

Greenpeace, 22 Columbo Street, London SE1.

Harriet Davis Seaside Holiday Trust for Disabled Children, 1 Bryncelyn Way, Llangynidr, Crickhowell, Powys NPB 1LY.

Health Education Council, 78 New Oxford Street, London WC1A 1AH.

Hindu Centre, 39 Grafton Terrace, London NW5.

Institute for the Study of Drug Dependence, 3 Blackburn Road, London NW6 1XX.

International Fund for Animal Welfare, Little Mead, Marsh Lane, Hartfield, East Sussex TN7 4ET.

International Society for the Protection of Animals, 106 Jermyn Street, London SW1.

Iona Community, Pearce Institute, 840 Govan Road, Glasgow G51 3UT.

Iona Community, Iona, Argyll PA76 6SN.

Islamic Cultural Centre, 146 Park Road, London NW8.

Israeli Government Office, 59 St James's Street, London SW1.

Jasperian Theatre Company, 29 Harvard Court, Honeybourne Road, London NW6 1HL.

Jewish Educational Bureau, 8 Westcombe Avenue, Leeds LS8 2BS.

Jewish Memorial Council Bookshop, 25 Enford Street, London W1.

Jewish Museum, The, 80 East End Road, Finchley, London N3 2SY.

Jewish National Fund, Harold Poster House, Kingsbury Circle, London NW9.

Kingsway Music, Lottbridge Drove, Eastbourne.

Langham Arts, St Paul's Church, Robert Adams St, London W1M 5AH.

Leprosy Mission International, The, 80 Windmill Road, Brentford, Middlesex TW8 0QH.

London Whale Watch, c/o Earl Lee, 53 Vicars Road, London NW5.

Look Hear!, c/o United Reformed Church, 86 Tavistock Place, London WC1H 9RT.

Lord Wharton's Charity, 30 Prentis Road, London SW16 1QD.

Lutheran World Federation, 150 route de Ferne, 1211 Geneva 20, Switzerland.

Men of the Trees, Crawley Downs, Crawley, Sussex RH10 4HL.

Methodist Association of Youth Clubs, 2 Chester House, Pages Lane, London N10 1PR.

Methodist Church: Division of Education and Youth, 2 Chester House, Pages Lane, London N10 1PR.

Methodist Church, Home Mission Division, 1 Central Buildings, Westminster, London SW1H 9NU.

Methodist Church, Overseas Division, 25–41 Marylebone Road, London NW1.

Methodist Publishing House, 20 Ivatt Way, Peterborough PE3 7PG.

Ministry of Overseas Development, Eland House, Stag Place, London SW1.

Mission to Seamen, St Michael Paternoster Royal, College Hill, London EC4R 2RL.

Muslim Information Service, 233 Seven Sisters Road, London N4.

National Association for Asian Youth, 46 High Street, Southall, Middlesex.

National Centre for Alternative Technology, Llwyngwern Quarry, Machynlleth, Powys, Gwynedd.

National Children's Home, 85 Highbury Park, London N5.

National Christian Education Council, 1020 Bristol Road, Selly Oak, Birmingham B29 6LB.

National Society (CE) for Promoting Religious Education, Church House, Great Smith Street, London SW1P 3NZ.

National Society's RE Centre, 36 Causton Street, London SW1P 4AU.

National Trust, The Old Grape House, Clivedon, Taplow, Maidenhead, Berks SL6 0HZ.

National Union of Journalists, 314 Grays Inn Road, London WC1X 8DP.

Nota Bene **Magazine**, Paternoster Press, Carlisle CA3 0QS.

Orbis International, PO Box 1685, London W8 4BR.

Oxfam Education Department, 274 Banbury Road, Oxford OX2 7DR.

Paraplegic Games, International Stoke Mandeville Games Federation, Harvey Road, Aylesbury, Bucks.

Parish Educational Publications (Church of Scotland), St Colm's, 20/23 Inverleith Terrace, Edinburgh EH3 5NS.

Peace Care, 39 Halsdon Road, Exmouth, Devon EX8 1SR.

People's Trust for Endangered Species, 19 Quarry Street, Guildford GU1 3HH.

Pictorial Charts Educational Trust, 27 Kitchen Road, London W13 0UD.

Pilgrim Homes, 175 Tower Bridge Road, London SE1 2AL.

Pioneer Centre, Cleobury Mortimer, Worcs DY14 8JG.

Quaker Home Service, Friends House, Euston Road, London NW1 2BJ.

RE Today, CEM, Royal Buildings, Victoria Street, Derby DE1 1GW.

Regional RE Centre, Westhill College, Wesley Park Rd, Selly Oak, Birmingham B29 6LL.

Release, 1 Elgin Avenue, London W9 3PR.

Religious and Moral Education Press, Chansitor Publications Ltd, St Mary's Works, St Mary's Plain, Norwich, NR3 3BH

Shelter, 88 Old Street, London EC1.

Stainer & Bell Ltd, PO Box 110 Victoria House, 23 Gruneisen Road, London N3 1DZ.

Royal National Lifeboat Institution, West Quay Road, Poole, Dorset BH15 1HZ.

Royal Mission to Deep Sea Fishermen, 43 Nottingham Place, London W1M 4BX.

Royal Society for the Prevention of Accidents, Cannon House, The Priory, Queensway, Birmingham B4 6BS.

Royal Society for the Prevention of Cruelty to Animals, The Causeway, Horsham, Sussex.

Royal Society for the Protection of Birds, The Lodge, Sandy, Beds.

Salvation Army, 101 Queen Victoria Street, London EC4P 4EP.

Save The Children Fund, Jebb House, 157 Clapham Road, London SW9 0PT.

School Worship File, 46 Latimer Road, Darlington, Co. Durham DL1 2AE.

Scout Association, Baden-Powell House, Queen's Gate, London SW7 5JS.

Scripture Union, 207 Queensway, Bletchley, Milton Keynes MK2 2EB.

Shaftesbury Society, 18–20 Kingston Road, London SW19 1JZ.

SHAP, West Sussex Institute of Higher Education, Bishop Otter College, Chichester, Sussex PO19 4PE.

Sikh Missionary Society, UK, 10 Featherstone Road, Southall, Middlesex.

Society for the Protection of the Unborn Child, 7 Tufton Street, London SW1P 3QN.

Soil Association, Walnut Tree Manor, Haughley, Stowmarket OP14 3TR.

St John Ambulance Brigade, Grosvenor Crescent, London SW1X 7EF.

St Paul Multimedia Productions UK, Middle Green, Langley, Slough, SL3 6BS.

Society for Promoting Christian Knowledge, Holy Trinity Church, Marylebone Road, London NW1 4DU.

Spring Harvest, 14 Horsted Square, Uckfield, East Sussex TN22 1QL.

TCAD Publications, 2 Mount Street, Manchester.

Tear Fund, 100 Church Road, Teddington, Middlesex TW11 8QE.

Theology, SPCK, Holy Trinity Church, Marylebone Road, London NW1 4DU.

Third Way **Journal**, St Peter's, Sumner Road, Harrow, Middlesex HA2 4BX.

UNICEF, 46–48 Osnaburgh Street, London NW1 3PU.

United Reformed Church, 86 Tavistock Place, London EC4 4EP.

United Society for the Propagation of the Gospel, 15 Tufton Street, London SW1P.

Vegetarian Society of the UK, Parkdale, Dunham Road, Altrincham, Cheshire WA14 4QG.

Veritas Book and Video Distribution Ltd, Lower Avenue, Leamington Spa, CV31 3NP.

Video Resource Unit—Central ITV, Attn. Head of Administration VRU, Central House, Broad Street, Birmingham B1 2JP.

Voluntary Committee on Overseas Aid and Development, Education Unit, Parnell House, 25 Wilton Road, London SW1.

War On Want, 467 Caledonian Road, London N7 9BE.

Westhill RE Centre, Westhill College, Selly Oak, Birmingham N29 6LL.

Wild Goose Publications, 840 Govan Road, Glasgow G51 3UT.

World Conference On Religion and Peace, 37 Grange Road, Bushey, Herts WD2 2LQ.

World Council of Churches, 150 route de Ferney, 1211 Geneva 20, Switzerland.

World Development Movement, Bedford Chambers, Covent Garden, London W2.

World Student Christian Federation, 2bis Auguste Vilbert, 1218 Grand-Saconnex, Switzerland.

World Wildlife Fund, 26 Grenville Street, London EC19.

World Young Women's Christian Association, 37 quai Ilson, 1201 Geneva, Switzerland.

ABBREVIATIONS

The following abbreviations have been used for reference throughout the book:

BCP	*Book of Common Prayer*
NEM	*New Every Morning* (BBC).
OBP	*The Oxford Book of Prayer*, ed. George Appleton, (OUP, 1985).
WCC	World Council of Churches
WE	*Worshipping Ecumenically*, ed. Per Harling (WCC, 1995).

WORSHIP MANUALS

This is a selective list of worship books, some of which are now out of print and only available as second-hand copies, that may be found useful in conjunction with the tenor, spirit, and content of this book.

A Wee Worship Book (Wild Goose Group).

All Desires Known, Janet Morley (SPCK, 1992).

At All Times and In All Places, Tony Jasper and Myra Blyth (Marshall Pickering, 1986).

Bread of Tomorrow, ed. Janet Morley (SPCK, 1992).

Come Holy Spirit: Renew The Whole Creation (WCC, 1989).

Community Worship, John J. Vincent (Ashram).

Contemporary Prayers: The Collected Edition, ed. Caryl Micklem (SCM, 1993).

Celebrating Together (Corrymeela Community).

Daily Office, revised, ed. Ronald C. Jasper (SPCK).

The Daily Service, ed. Lavinia Byrne (Hodder and Stoughton, 1998)

Echoes of Our Journey, Dorothy McRae McMahon (JBCE, Australia, 1993, 1994).

Edge Of Glory, David Adam (Triangle, 1985, 1988).

Everyday Prayers, Allen Birtwhistle, Bernard Thorogood, and Michael Walker (International Bible Reading Association, 1978).

Feeding On God, Shelagh Brown (Bible Reading Fellowship, 1995).

Hello! This Is Message . . . ed. Diana Newlands.

I Hear a Seed Growing—God of the Streets, Edwina Gateley (Anthony Clarke, 1990).

In Unexpected Places, Tony Jasper and Myra Blyth (Harper Collins, 1988).

Interpreted By Love, collected by Elizabeth Basset (1994).

Iona Community Worship Book (Wild Goose Publications, 1987, 1991).

Liturgy of Life, Donald Hilton (NCEC, 1991).

Living Prayers for Today, Maureen Edwards (IBRA).

Living Words for Now, Tony Jasper (SPCK).

Lord Of All, Hear Our Prayer, Ted Burge (Canterbury Press, 1991).

New Glory, ed. Brian Frost (BBC, 1979).

No More Strangers (Movement for the Ordination of Women).

Oxford Book of Prayer, ed. George Appleton (OUP, 1985).

Praise In All Our Days (Common prayers at Taizé) (Mowbray).

Prayer In The Morning, Jim Cotter (Cairns Publications, 1989, 1990).

Prayers for People in Hospital, Neville Smith (OUP, 1994).

Prayers for People in Prison, William Noblett (OUP, 1998).

Prayers for the Church Community, Roy Chapman and Donald Hilton (NCEC, 1978, 1996).

Sing and Pray and Shout Hurray! compiled by Roger Ortmayer (Friendship, USA).

Sounds of Fury, compiled by Donald Hilton (United Reformed Church, 1994).

Tides and Seasons, David Adam (Triangle, 1989).

With All God's People, compiled by John Carden (WCC, 1989, 1990).

Women of Prayer, Dorothy M. Stewart (Lion, 1993).

Woman Prayer Woman Song, Miriam Theresa Winter (Crossroad, USA, 1991, 1996).

Women Included, St Hilda Community (SPCK).

Worshipping Ecumenically, ed. Per Harling (WCC Publications, 1995).

Your Word Is Near, Hubb Oosterhuis (Fowler Wright).

POETRY

This is by no means an exhaustive list of recent published work in which there can be found material that relates to the themes found in this book. There is a Christian or a general religious orientation to many of the titles listed.

Carter, Sydney, *Nothing Fixed Or Final* (Galliard, 1969).

Casley, Martin, *Hands On Angels* (Stride, 1992).

Claydon, Graham, *Islington 7* (Sea Dream, 1987).

Clegg, Arthur: *Pictures of the Thirties* (Reality, 1975).

Clemo Jack, *Approach To Murano* (Bloodaxe, 1993).

Clemo, Jack, *Banner Poems* (Cornish Nationalist Publications, 1989).

Clemo, Jack, *Selected Poems* (Bloodaxe, 1988).

Clemo, Jack, *The Cured Arno* (Bloodaxe, 1995).

Davis, Michael Justin, *To The Cross* (SPCK, 1991).

Donne, John, *Masters Of Prayer* (Church Publishing House, 1984).

Eliot, T. S., *The Waste Land and Other Poems* (Faber & Faber, 1940).

Galloway, Kathy, *Love Burning Deep* (SPCK, 1993).

Harding, David J., *Peace Poems* (Peace Care, 1990).

Henderson, Stewart, *A Giant's Scrapbook* (Spire, 1989).

Henderson, Stewart, *Whose Idea of Fun is a Nightmare?* (Musical Gospel Outreach, 1975).

Kamntaris, Sylvia, *Lad's Love* (Bloodaxe, 1993).

Keay, Kathy, *Laughter, Silence and Shouting* (Harper Collins, 1994).

Law, Mags, *Nets Full Of Holes* (Sea Dream, 1991).

Loydell, Robert, *Between Dark Dreams* (Acumen, 1992).

Palmer, Graham, *If The Face Fits* (Stride, 1984).

Patterson, Evangeline, *Lucifer At The Fair* (Stride, 1992).

Ratushinskaya, Irina, *No, I'm Not Afraid* (Bloodaxe, 1987).

Rumble, Coral, *Select Few* (Sea Dream, 1993).

Smith, Stevie, *Selected Poems*, ed. James MacGibbon (Penguin, 1975).

Taylor, Cecily, *Contact* (Galliard, 1972).

Turner, Steve, *Up To Date* (Hodder & Stoughton, 1976).

Turner, Steve, *Twists and Turns of Life* (Hodder & Stoughton, 1992).

Velvart, M., *At A Peculiar Angle* (Sea Dream, 1994).

Wright, Judith, *Phantom Feeling* (Virago, 1986).

ANTHOLOGIES

100 Contemporary Christian Poets, compiled by Gordon Bailey (Lion, 1983).

Early English Poets, ed. Ruth Etchells (Lion, 1988).

Faith in Her Words: Six Centuries of Women's Poetry, ed. Veronica Zundell (Lion, 1991).

Ghetto: Poems from a Warsaw Ghetto, ed. Jenny Robertson (Lion, 1990).

Interpreted By Love, compiled by Elizabeth Basset (Darton, Longman & Todd, 1994).

The Lion Book of Christian Poetry, compiled by Pat Alexander (Lion, 1981).

The Lion Christian Poetry Collection, compiled by Mary Batchelor (Lion, 1995).

Making Eden Grow, compiled by Colin Duriez (Scripture Union, 1974).

The New Younger Irish Poets, ed. Gerald Dawe (Blackstaff Press, 1982).

Poetry With An Edge, ed. Neil Astley (Bloodaxe, 1988).

Pushing The Boat Out, ed. Kathy Galloway (Wild Goose, 1995).

A Touch Of Flame, compiled by Jenny Robertson (Lion, 1989).

A Treasury of Christian Verse, ed. Hugh Martin (SCM, 1959).

Visions Of Glory, compiled by William Sykes (Bible Reading Fellowship, 1995).

Voices, series, ed. Geoffrey Summerfield (Penguin, various published dates).

MUSIC

Within the service outlines in this book are suggestions for appropriate hymns and worship songs. These have been selected from *BBC Songs of Praise* (OUP/BBC, 1997), a compilation of the best traditional hymns and contemporary Christian music. Worship leaders will need to draw from a wider range of material as new patterns for worship are developed, and there are numerous collections available.

In addition to the BBC hymnbook, and its successor, *Broadcast Praise*, there are the mainstream denominational hymnbooks, *Baptist Praise and Worship*, *Church Hymnary*, *Celebration Hymnal*, *Hymns Ancient and Modern*, *Hymns and Psalms*, *Songs of Praise*, *Congregational Praise*, *Redemption Hymnal*, *Grace*, *Making Melody*, *Rejoice and Sing*, *The English Hymnal*, and *With One Voice*.

The 'praise movement' has spawned countless general hymn and songbooks, with most major 'praise gatherings' producing their own material. The list includes some of these titles, and among the others there are some that should, in the view of the compiler, be better known.

Alleluya! compilation by David Gadsby and John Hoggarth (A. C. Black).

Big Blue Planet (Stainer and Bell/Methodist Publishing House, 1996).

Celebrating Community (WCC). (This volume includes worship material.)

The Complete Come and Praise, compiled by Geoffrey Marshall Taylor (BBC Books, 1990).

Gentle Angry People: Songs of Protest and Praise (Alliance of Radical Methodists).

Gloria Deo (Conference of European Churches). (This volume includes worship material.)

Hymns for Today's Church (Hodder & Stoughton, 1982, 1987).

Hymns of Faith (Scripture Union, 1964).

Hymns of the City, ed. John Vincent (Ashram Community).

In Spirit and in Truth, Hymns and Responses (WCC, 1991).

Jesus Praise (Scripture Union, 1981).

Let's Praise (Marshall Pickering, 1988, 1994).

Love from Below (Wild Goose Publications, 1989).

Mission Praise, vol. 1, 2, and 3 combined (Marshall Pickering, 1990).

Partners In Praise (Chester House Publications, 1979).

Songs of Fellowship for Kids (Kingsway).

Songs of Worship (Scripture Union, 1980).

Sound the Bamboo (CAA Hymnal).

Taizé Chants (Taizé Community).

Wild Goose Songs vol. 1 (Wild Goose Publications, 1987).

Wild Goose Songs vol. 2 (Wild Goose Publications, 1988).

Worship Songs Ancient and Modern (Canterbury Press, 1992).

ACKNOWLEDGEMENTS

Every effort has been made to trace the owners of material used in this book. The editors gratefully acknowledge the permission given by the following for permission to reproduce copyright material. If any material has not been correctly acknowledged, the publishers will willingly correct this in the first available reprint.

The Scripture quotations contained herein are from *The New Revised Standard Version of the Bible, Anglicized Edition*, copyright © 1989, 1995 by the Division of Christian Education of the National Council of the Churches of Christ in the United States of America, and are used by permission. All rights reserved.

BBC Books; for permission to use extracts from *New Every Morning*.

Coventry Cathedral; for permission to use an extract from the *Liturgy of Reconciliation*.

The London Ecumenical AIDS Trust; for permission to use the prayer 'Turn Your Spirit Loose' on page 2, adapted from a Native American prayer.

Macmillan Publishers Ltd; for permission to use 'Fruit Gathering' from *Collected Poems and Plays* by Rabindranath Tagore on page 76.

SCM Press Ltd; Anonymous, 'From Jaini-Bi–With Love' in *Voices of Women: An Asian Anthology* ed. Alison O'Grady (Singapore: Asian Christian Women's Conference 1978). Quoted in *Struggle to be the Sun Again*, page 72 by Chung Hyun Kyung, SCM Press 1991.

The Waldensian Church; for permission to use material from *The Waldensian Liturgy* on page 94.

The Very Reverend Professor James Whyte; for permission to use the prayer 'Across the Barriers' on page 101 from *Worship Now*, published by the St. Andrew's Press.

The World Alliance of Reformed Churches; for permission to use a poem by Hsu T'en Hsien on page 64 from *Testimonies of Faith: Letters and Poems from Prison in Taiwan*.

The World Council of Churches; for permission to use 'O bless this people, Lord' on page 109, from *Let's Worship 1975*.